AF321945

"To be able to wrestle with the legacy of Thomas Aquinas, we must take seriously his vocation as reader and teacher of Holy Scripture. John Boyle's accessible manuscript helps convey his principles and introduce the reader to a litany of case studies. It's a wonderful entryway to Thomas as exegete and master of the sacred page."

MICHAEL ALLEN
Reformed Theological Seminary

"John Boyle's *Aquinas on Scripture* is the clearest, most succinct, and most satisfying introduction to Thomas Aquinas's comprehensive vision of Scripture that I have had the privilege of reading. Accessible, lucid, and written in a deceptively simple style, Boyle's explication participates in *claritas* in which Thomas thinks and with which he teaches. I warmly recommend this book to every lover of the Holy Scriptures and to every student of Thomas Aquinas's thought, especially of his exegetical commentaries."

REINHARD HÜTTER
The Catholic University of America

"It is a joy to commend this volume. You will sense yourself in the hands of a master, and so you are. This comes through in the form of gentle wisdom, clarity of thought, a concern to be understood. And this flows from his overriding concern: that St. Thomas be understood, in the ways and habits that make him an interpreter of Sacred Scripture. That this is accomplished in the scope of a compact introduction makes it all the more winsome."

CHRISTOPHER SEITZ
Wycliffe College in the University of Toronto

"John Boyle unpacks Thomas Aquinas's thinking about biblical interpretation with clarity and conciseness, using the journalist's questions—who? what? why? how?—to describe Thomas's attempt to understand biblical texts in terms of efficient, material, final, and formal 'causes,' that themselves correspond to the author, subject matter, purpose, and literary genres of Scripture respectively. The goal is to understand the truths Scripture is communicating necessary for salvation: glorious life with God forever. In an age dominated by the conflict of interpretation theories, Boyle's commentary on Aquinas's commentary is a model of its kind, an essay in aid in understanding Thomas and the Scriptures that were the objects of his undivided holy attention."

KEVIN J. VANHOOZER
Trinity Evangelical Divinity School

"Long before the term 'biblical Thomism' was coined and the perspective on Thomas Aquinas as a biblical theologian became one of the most fruitful ways to engage with St. Thomas's thought, John Boyle was already laying its groundwork. And so by demonstrating time and again that St. Thomas was first and foremost an interpreter of Sacred Scripture who brings an extraordinary clarity and precision to the text, John Boyle became the dean of a whole generation of biblical Thomists in the United States. After the publication of a collection of his academic articles in 2021 (*The Order and Division of Divine Truth: St. Thomas Aquinas as Scholastic Master of the Sacred Page*), Boyle now offers a 'little book' on how St. Thomas read and understood Sacred Scripture, meant as an accessible introduction. But it takes a master in medieval biblical exegesis and a precise expositor of St. Thomas like Boyle to introduce the reader into the often complex dynamics of St. Thomas's engagement with Scripture. Boyle's approach shows him to be an excellent pedagogue as well. The first chapter introduces the reader into the hermeneutical assumptions often implicit in St. Thomas's text. The remainder of the book uses the fourfold way in which one asks questions why? who? what? how? in order to shed light on what St. Thomas tells us about the usefulness (why?), author (who?), subject matter (what?), and the literary style (how?) of Sacred Scripture. All this is richly illustrated with examples from St. Thomas's Old and New Testament commentaries.

This book is absolutely unique in its kind because its composition requires the level of knowledge, skills, and love for Sacred Scripture and St. Thomas's reading of it which John Boyle continuously displayed over the years. It could not, also, come at a better time when Aquinas's biblical writings are receiving a new readership and are being explored for their clarity and richness. It should be required reading for anyone engaging St. Thomas or Scripture and deserves to be placed on one's bookshelf next to introductions to St. Thomas by Boyle's illustrious colleagues like Chenu, Weisheipl, and Torrell."

JÖRGEN VIJGEN
Pontifical Academy of Saint Thomas

"A new wave of important studies is emerging on St. Thomas Aquinas as an interpreter and commentator of Scripture. How did the medievals interpret Scripture as a text containing divine revelation, and what role did philosophical learning and clear theological reasoning play in this process? John Boyle is at the vanguard of these recent studies, and this book helps greatly to advance our understanding of theology as *sacra doctrina*: the study and interpretation of holy scripture, providing human beings with speculative and saving knowledge of God."

THOMAS JOSEPH WHITE, OP
Pontifical University of St. Thomas Aquinas, *Angelicum*

Reading Scripture within the Tradition

AQUINAS ON SCRIPTURE

A Primer

AQUINAS ON SCRIPTURE

A Primer

JOHN F. BOYLE

EMMAUS
ACADEMIC

Steubenville, Ohio
www.emmausacademic.com

EMMAUS
ACADEMIC

Steubenville, Ohio
www.emmausacademic.com

A Division of The St. Paul Center for Biblical Theology
Editor-in-Chief: Scott Hahn
1468 Parkview Circle
Steubenville, Ohio 43952

Library of Congress Cataloging-in-Publication Data
Names: Boyle, John F., 1958- author.
Title: Aquinas on scripture : a primer / John F. Boyle.
Description: Steubenville, Ohio : Emmaus Academic, 2023. |
   Summary: "With precision and profundity born of 30 years of devoted study, John Boyle offers an essential introduction to St. Thomas Aquinas on Scripture, shedding helpful light on the goals, methods, and commitments that animate the Angelic Doctor's engagement with the sacred page. Because the genius of St. Thomas's approach to the Bible lies not so much in its novelty but rather in the fidelity and clarity with which he recapitulates the riches of the preceding interpretive Tradition, this initiation into St. Thomas's vision of Scripture is itself an orientation to the Church's vision of Scripture, from the Fathers through and beyond the Middle Ages. St. Thomas's embeddedness within the Church's Tradition and his own historical context is integral to his approach to Scripture, yet it sets him at some distance from modern readers, for whom his interpretive vision may seem perplexing or even impenetrable. In this Primer, Boyle first provides an acclimation to this medieval context through a survey and explanation of pertinent technical terminology used by St. Thomas and characteristic of the scholastic theology of the time. With an eye to the medieval practice of considering Scripture according to the fourfold division of causes, Boyle builds on this initial foundation by exploring in turn St. Thomas's accounts of the end or use of Scripture (final cause), its divine and human authorship (efficient cause), its order and division (material cause), and its literary styles or genres (formal cause). Drawing on writings from across St. Thomas's corpus, but especially his work On the Commendation and Division of Sacred Scripture and the prologues to his biblical commentaries, Boyle masterfully elucidates both the hermeneutical principles and deep wisdom of the Angelic Doctor's approach to Scripture, imparting invaluable guidance not only for reading and understanding St. Thomas and other great masters of the Tradition, but also-and ultimately-for understanding Scripture in light of this Tradition and reading it with greater benefit and joy"-- Provided by publisher.
Identifiers: LCCN 2022053129 (print) | LCCN 2022053130 (ebook) | ISBN 9781645852650 (hardcover) | ISBN 9781645852667 (paperback) | ISBN 9781645852674 (ebook)
Subjects: LCSH: Thomas, Aquinas, Saint, 1225?-1274. | Bible--Criticism, interpretation, etc. | Theology, Doctrinal--History--Middle Ages,

Cover design by Allison Merrick
Layout by Laura Cruise

Cover image: Saint Thomas Aquinas, Studio of Bartolomé Esteban Murillo (Seville 1618–1682), Private collection.

To Dia

Table of Contents

CITATIONS AND ABBREVIATIONS

As the translations from St. Thomas are my own, the citations are to the Latin text. I provide citation to St. Thomas's internal division first and then citation to the Latin edition as needed. The translations of Sacred Scripture are from St. Thomas's Latin.

I have used three different editions of the works of St. Thomas:

Leonine ed.	*Opera omnia* (Rome: Leonine Commission, 1882–). The Leonine edition of the works of Thomas Aquinas was commissioned by Pope Leo XIII. The volumes that have appeared since the second half of the twentieth century provide the best critically edited texts of St. Thomas's work. Much remains to be published. Of his Scripture commentaries, only the commentaries on Job and Isaiah have been published to date in this edition. Citations are to volume number and page number, e.g. Leonine ed., 28:4.
Marietti ed.	Editions of the works of Thomas Aquinas published by Marietti in Turin. I use Marietti editions for St. Thomas's commentaries on the New Testament. Most Marietti editions have their own internal paragraph numbering, which has been widely adopted in citing the works of St. Thomas; these numbers often appear now in English translations. Citations are to paragraph number, e.g. Marietti no. 345.

| Parma ed. | *Opera Omnia* (Parma: Fiaccadori, 1852–1873). I have used the Parma edition for St. Thomas's commentaries on the Psalms, Jeremiah, and Lamentations. The Parma edition provides its own paragraph numbers, except for the prologues. Citations are to volume number, page number, and, where applicable, paragraph number. For example: Parma ed., 14:151, no. 3. |

Citations to St. Thomas's Scripture commentaries:

I cite St. Thomas's commentaries by the specific book of Scripture followed by the modern chapter and verse numbering of the book.

St. Thomas divides his New Testament commentaries into *lectiones*; in citing these commentaries, I note the *lectio* number for the particular chapter. The Marietti paragraph number then follows. For example: *Super Rom* 9:15, lec. 3, Marietti no. 769.

Abbreviations for individual works:

Catena aurea	*Catena aurea in quatuor evangelia*, edited by A. Guarienti, 2 vols. (Marietti ed., 1953).
De commendatione	*De commendatione et partitione Sacrae Scripturae*, in *Opuscula theologica*, edited by R. Verardo, 2 vols. (Marietti ed., 1954), vol. 1, pp. 435–39, nos. 1199–1208.
De potentia	*Quaestiones disputatae de potentia* in *Quaestiones disputatae*, edited by P. Pession et al., 8th ed., 2 vols. (Marietti ed., 1949), vol. 2, pp. 7–275. Citations are to question number, article number, and article section when relevant.
In Jer	*In Jeremiam prophetam expositio* (Parma ed., 1863), vol. 14, pp. 577–667.
In Psalmos	*In Psalmos Davidis expositio* (Parma ed., 1863), vol. 14, pp. 148–353.
In Thren	*In Threnos Jeremiae expositio* (Parma ed., 1863), vol. 14, pp. 668–85.
Quodlibet	*Quaestiones quodlibetales* (Leonine ed., 1996), vol. 25. Citation are to quodlibet number (I–XII), question number, article number, and article section when relevant.

SCG	*Summa contra gentiles* (Leonine ed., 1918–1930), vols. 13–15. Citations are to book number and chapter number.
ST	*Summa theologiae* (Ottawa: Commissio Piana, 1953), commonly known as the "Ottawa *Summa*." Citations are to part number (I, I-II, II-II, III), question number, article number, and article section when relevant.
Super 2 Tim	*Super secundam epistolam ad Timotheum lectura*, in *Super epistolas s. Pauli lectura*, edited by R. Cai, 8th ed., 2 vols. (Marietti ed., 1953), vol. 2, pp. 265–99.
Super Gal	*Super epistolam ad Galatas lectura* in *Super epistolas s. Pauli lectura*, edited by R. Cai, 8th ed., 2 vols. (Marietti ed., 1953), vol. 1, pp. 563–639.
Super Heb	*Super epistolam ad Hebraeos lectura* in *Super epistolas s. Pauli lectura*, edited by R. Cai, 8th ed., 2 vols. (Marietti ed., 1953), vol. 2, pp. 335–506.
Super Ioan	*Super evangelium s. Ioannis lectura*, edited by R. Cai (Marietti ed., 1952).
Super Iob	*Expositio super Iob ad litteram* (Leonine ed., 1965), vol. 26.
Super Isa	*Expositio super Isaiam ad litteram* (Leonine ed., 1974), vol. 28.
Super Matt	*Super evangelium s. Matthaei lectura*, edited by R. Cai, 5th ed. (Marietti ed., 1951).
Super Rom	*Super epistolam ad Romanos Lectura* in *Super epistolas s. Pauli lectura*, edited by R. Cai, 8th ed., 2 vols. (Marietti ed., 1953), vol. 1, pp. 5–230.

In the case of St. Thomas's commentary on the letters of St. Paul, I cite his general prologue to the whole commentary thus: *Super epistolas s. Pauli*, prol., Marietti nos. 1–10.

INTRODUCTION

This little book is an introduction to how St. Thomas Aquinas read and understood Sacred Scripture. I hope it will be accessible to anyone interested in St. Thomas as a reader of Sacred Scripture. I do not presume any particular knowledge of St. Thomas on the part of my reader.

Of all the figures in the Catholic tradition, why St. Thomas? One could answer that St. Thomas, as the Common Doctor, has a privileged place among the Church's teachers. This is true, but we can pursue this a bit further. In the case of Sacred Scripture, St. Thomas exquisitely exemplifies the tradition of the Church. In his fundamental understanding of Sacred Scripture, St. Thomas has nothing particularly novel to say. He reflects the tradition of the Fathers, whom he read assiduously, as he also reflects what is best in the thinking of the Middle Ages. What St. Thomas brings to his thinking on Sacred Scripture is his extraordinary clarity and precision of mind. His ability to articulate the foundations of the tradition's thinking on Scripture are, to my mind, second to none.

Thus, in understanding St. Thomas, one can come to understand much of the tradition. It is not that St. Thomas interprets a given verse of Scripture in the same way as St. Augustine or St. John Chrysostom or St. Bernard; rather, he approaches Scripture in essentially the same way. The *principles* are the same; the ways of engaging Scripture are the same. What St. Thomas has to offer is a particularly clear *articulation* of this. The fact is that the tradition is remarkably uniform in its foundations, and thus there is not extensive writing on the part of the Fathers or the medieval thinkers on what we might now call the "hermeneutical" or "interpretive" questions surrounding Scripture. What was clear to them is not necessarily clear to us, often so far removed from their common understanding of Scripture, and thus we can find it difficult to understand how and why they interpret Scripture as they do.

St. Thomas is a particularly fruitful thinker for getting at the principles and insights that govern that most glorious tradition of interpretating Scripture, from the Fathers through and beyond the Middle Ages. If we can better understand these foundational principles and insights, we can read the commentaries not only of St. Thomas but of the great masters of the tradition with benefit and joy.

I have, thus, set myself the task of helping interested readers understand Sacred Scripture as St. Thomas does. How does he understand Scripture in its sweep and in its detail? How does he read it? These are the questions of this book. My intention is to enter into the mind of St. Thomas, to understand his language and his lines of thought so that he might teach us how he reads Scripture.

In his voluminous writings, St. Thomas has little to say in a systematic way about interpreting Scripture. He just sets about reading it. He can do this because, in the end, he has nothing new to say. He can thus presume a lot of his reader, and this can be a source of great frustration and confusion for his modern readers. Indeed, a similar frustration greets many modern readers hoping to read the Fathers or the masters of the Middle Ages. For this reason, the first chapter of this book is precisely about what St. Thomas presumes of his reader.

In trying to think with St. Thomas, I have sought to bring out his own categories that illuminate his thinking and his writing, especially as an interpreter of Sacred Scripture. At the heart of St. Thomas's thinking are "causes," which is a way of saying a set of basic human questions: why?, who?, what?, and how? In the Middle Ages these questions were applied to books, and they shape St. Thomas's work as a commentator. The second chapter briefly presents these questions as used by St. Thomas the commentator.

The remainder of the book then pursues each of these questions, each of these causes, as St. Thomas uses them. I have tried to make use of his explicit considerations of these questions, which are found most frequently and fully in his prologues to his commentaries, as well as periodic examples from his commentaries. My goal is always to understand St. Thomas in his own terms and in such a way as to make those terms intelligible to a modern reader. I will have succeeded if the reader of this book is able to read St. Thomas and other great commentators in the tradition fruitfully and with joy—indeed even better if they are able to read Scripture itself with greater fruitfulness and joy.

A final note on what this book is not. It is not a survey of St. Thomas's commentaries on Scripture, their place in his intellectual biography, or their textual histories. Nor is it a guide to the growing scholarly literature on St. Thomas's commentaries. Such is beyond the modest scope of this book. The interested reader can find all of this readily enough elsewhere.

CHAPTER I

WHAT THOMAS PRESUMES OF HIS READER

Before we consider the specifics of St. Thomas as a commentator on Sacred Scripture, we need to consider a number of things that St. Thomas more or less presumes that his reader knows and that are important for us to know as well.

Words

Let us begin with words. For Thomas, words, whether spoken or written, are signs. They do something: they signify; they point. To what do they point? They point to ideas in our minds. Those ideas in our minds in turn have their own signifying task, pointing to things outside the mind. Thus, the word "dog" signifies the idea of dog in my mind and in yours, which ideas, in turn, ultimately signify real dogs, whether playing with children in the backyard or chewing bones before the fire. That last step matters because it ultimately grounds the possibility that we might actually be having a conversation in which we are both speaking of the same thing. Words signify by convention, meaning by agreement of those speaking. If one is not part of the convention, one does not understand: the words do not function as signs; they are merely sounds. Such is the frustrating experience of the traveler in a foreign land who does not speak the language.

Sensus

In English, we do not typically speak of a word's "signification," but rather its "meaning." In Latin that would be the *sensus* of the word. *Sensus* is a rich word in Latin, just as "sense" is in English. We speak of a particular sense or meaning of a word, and *sensus* can be understood in this sense, as the meaning of a word. St. Thomas will also speak of the sense of a phrase or a sentence, as in English we might speak of a bit of prose "making sense" or not.

Oratio

The grammatical unit of the sentence is for St. Thomas an *oratio*, a grammatically complete unit made up of words.[1] It may or may not express a complete idea. Often we need several sentences to present something of a complete idea; any given sentence in this context is an incomplete idea.

---

[1] Not to be confused with another sense of *oratio* meaning "prayer."

Sententia

Our English word "sentence" comes from the Latin *sententia*, but we want to be careful not to confuse *sententia* with "sentence" as a grammatically complete unit. That is *oratio*. *Sententia* can refer to the grammatical unit, but more commonly for Thomas it refers to a complete thought that might well be made up of several *orationes* (grammatically complete sentences). St. Thomas works to articulate the *sententia* of an author, and by that he generally means a thought. It is possible to take *sententia* as "meaning," but with the precision of a complete thought or idea.[2]

The most famous theological textbook of the high Middle Ages is Peter Lombard's *Liber sententiarum*, the *Book of Sentences*. It is a kind of theological commonplace book, consisting principally of quotations from the Fathers arranged by topic. "Quotation" does not, however, quite get at it. Peter was not producing a book of familiar theological quotations; he was producing a book of theological ideas, the essential and defining ideas of the Fathers. Those ideas expressed in words are quite properly *sententiae*; hence, the *Book of Sentences*.

In his *Catena aurea*, St. Thomas brings together quotations from the Fathers to comment verse by verse on all four Gospels. He refers to those quotations as *sententiae*, the thoughts of the Fathers on specific passages of the Gospels.[3] In his commentary on Job, St. Thomas sees the dispute between Job and his

---

[2] There is another meaning of *sententia* in Latin corresponding to the English "sentence" as the punishment given by a judge in a court. This meaning of *sententia* is particularly present, not surprisingly, in St. Thomas's commentaries on Isaiah and Jeremiah.

[3] In *Catena aurea*, see the *epistola dedicatoria* on Matthew and the *epistola dedicatoria* on Mark (Marietti ed., vol. 1, pp. 4 and 429, respectively).

friends as a dispute over *sententiae*. He can speak of the *sententia* of Eliphaz, referring to the totality of his argument and its attendant reasons for the sinfulness of Job. In turn, Job's understanding of providence is a contrary *sententia*.[4]

The task of the commentator then is to make sense of the author's words. His task is to understand the signification of the words in order to figure out their meaning (*sensus*) so as to see how they constitute a coherent idea (*sententia*). This is, one would like to think, what any commentator on any book is striving to do.

Sacred Scripture

Littera

Sacred Scripture is a written text. Thomas speaks of the "letter" (*littera*), by which he means in great part what we mean by "text," something written. Scripture, for St. Thomas, was in Latin translation. He had no working knowledge of the original Greek or Hebrew. The Latin translation, known as the Vulgate, was relatively stable in St. Thomas's day. Thomas calls it "our letter." He knew there were other translations. Bits and pieces of the various Old Latin translations survived in the works of the Fathers. Thomas also knows of the Septuagint, the Jewish translation of the Old Testament from Hebrew into Greek in the first century BC, and he knew that the Greek can differ from the Hebrew and that those differences could make their way into the Latin translations. He notes that, when St. Paul quotes Exodus in his letter to the Romans, he uses a "different

---

[4] In *Super Iob*, see, e.g., on Job 8:1 (Leonine ed., 26:52); 14:7 (26:52); 14:18 (26:94).

letter," a different translation, meaning the Septuagint, and not "our letter."[5]

The Psalter circulated in three different versions in the Middle Ages, and St. Thomas was aware of all three.[6] St. Thomas referred to St. Jerome's revision of the Old Latin as the "Italian" version; it is now known as the "Roman Psalter," as it found its way into the Roman missal. St. Jerome undertook a second revision based on the Septuagint that was adopted by Alcuin in the ninth-century Carolingian efforts to establish a sound text of the Vulgate. As a result, St. Thomas called it the French version; it is now known as the "Gallican Psalter." It is this version of the Psalms that is, for St. Thomas, "our letter." St. Jerome undertook a third translation directly from the Hebrew, sometimes referred to as the *iuxta Hebraeos*. St. Thomas knew it and also reported that it was not sung in any church; in other words, unlike the other two translations, it had no liturgical use. St. Thomas contrasted Jerome (i.e., the *iuxta Hebraeos*) with "our letter," meaning the Gallican Psalter in the Vulgate.[7]

"Letter" and "meaning" (*sensus*) are not the same. There could be two translations, two letters, but in fact with the same meaning.[8] We see the distinction at work in Thomas's commentary on Matthew. After Peter's profession of faith, Christ instructs his apostles to tell no one that he is the Christ. St. Thomas asks a question raised by the Fathers: if Jesus has earlier

---

[5] *Super Rom* 9:15, lec. 3, Marietti no. 769.

[6] *In Psalmos*, prooemium (Parma ed., 14:149).

[7] For example, *In Psalmos* 7:10 (Parma ed., 14:165, no. 5; second pagination sequence, as the edition has a repetition of page numbers).

[8] See *Super Heb* 12:26, lec. 5, Marietti no. 720, where St. Thomas notes that the text of Haggai quoted by Paul is not the same as that found in the Vulgate translation ("our letter"), but having noted this, he simply concludes "the meaning [*sensus*] is the same."

commanded his apostles to preach the Kingdom of God, why does he now prohibit it? Before turning to the substantive answers of the Fathers, St. Thomas says that the question might be answered in this way: he had earlier commanded them to announce not Christ but the Kingdom of God. This is, says St. Thomas, according to the "surface of the letter." It is strictly speaking what the letter says: Kingdom of God in Matthew 10 and Jesus Christ in Matthew 16. From the vantage point of the letter, there is no problem. From the vantage point of meaning, however, there is. Because the proclamation of the Kingdom of God includes in itself the proclamation of Christ, it would follow that what he commanded in Matthew 10 he forbids in Matthew 16. The surface of the letter suggests a distinction that could answer the question, but when one considers what the words signify, when one considers their meaning, then one can see that the initial answer is according to the "surface" of the text. How fitting that we get our word "superficial" from the Latin word for surface that Thomas uses here.[9]

The Perfection of Scripture

Sacred Scripture is, for the Christian, unlike any other book. This is obvious enough, and it is worth considering how St. Thomas describes that uniqueness. St. Thomas has left us a short work that in its modern edition is fittingly enough entitled *De commendatione et partitione Sacrae Scripturae*—On the Commendation and Division of Sacred Scripture.[10] It is a work

---

[9] *Super Matt* 16:20, lec. 3, Marietti no. 1394.

[10] The work was discovered in the twentieth century and there has been discussion as to its authenticity. It strikes me as authentic, but even apart from that, the ideas expressed in it are quite consonant with St. Thomas's thinking.

that can be helpful for understanding the implications of the distinctiveness of Scripture for St. Thomas.

In it, St. Thomas speaks of the perfection of Scripture, which he commends in three ways: in its *authority*, its *truth*, and its *usefulness*. The first of these ways, Scripture's *authority*, is itself manifest in three things. (1) The authority of Scripture is established in its very origin, which is God, who in his nature is truth itself, who has the perfect fullness of knowledge, and whose very words are efficacious. (2) The authority of Scripture applies to the fullness of the Christian life, as its commandments direct the intellect through faith, inform the affections through love, and move the believer to act. (3) The authority of Scripture is manifest in the uniformity of its teachings, because all who hand on the sacred teaching teach the same things.[11]

In St. Thomas's second way of speaking of its perfection, the *truth* of the teaching of Scripture is immutable and eternal. This is so because of the power and immutability of the divine legislator.[12]

Third, St. Thomas finds the perfection of Scripture in the fact that it is more *useful* than anything else, for all who hold to it come to the life of grace to which Scripture disposes, to the life of justice in works to which Scripture directs, and finally to the life of glory that Scripture promises and to which it leads.[13]

Scripture is, simply, perfect. That perfection follows from its author, God. It is perfect in the truth it teaches and the way of life it commands. It is perfect in disposing man to new life here and in eternal glory. Bold claims for a book.

---

[11] *De commendatione*, Marietti no. 1200.
[12] *De commendatione*, Marietti no. 1201.
[13] *De commendatione*, Marietti no. 1202.

The Senses of Scripture

The most famous, or notorious, feature of the medieval inter-pretation of Scripture is the multiplicity of "senses." The senses of Scripture abound, and even their number is subject to change. The Latin is *sensus*. We noted above that *sensus* can be taken to refer to the meaning of a word. Let us pursue *sensus* a bit further. In its primary meaning, *sensus* and its English deriv-ative "sense" refer to the powers by which we perceive certain aspects of the world. We speak of the "sense of sight" by which we perceive color. "Sense" is a power of perception. Taking the word a step further, we wonder "in what sense" something is to be understood. Here "sense" refers to the particular vantage point from which we understand what someone says. Just as we perceive something from the vantage point of color by means of the sense of sight, we can speak of perceiving what someone says from a particular vantage point, "in some sense" such that it is intelligible or understandable.

In approaching the senses of Scripture, "sense" here speaks to the particular vantage point from which one approaches the letter. It is the way by which one approaches Scripture so as to get at what the words signify, and thereby to the *sententia* (the idea) of the author. Thus, St. Thomas often indicates the senses adverbially: he will speak of reading the letter "literally" or "mystically," by which he means according to the literal sense or the mystical sense. "Sense" speaks to the approach to the letter or text at hand. In the case of Scripture this is particularly wild, for there are multiple senses.

For St. Thomas, the fundamental division of the senses of Scripture is between the "literal" or "historical," on the one hand, and the "spiritual" or "mystical," on the other. He uses "literal" and "historical" interchangeably, as he does "spiritual" and "mystical." What is the difference between the two? The difference, in principle, is remarkably simple. The literal sense of Scripture refers to what things the words signify. The spiritual sense refers to what things are further signified—not by the words of Scripture, but rather further signified by the things signified by the words of Scripture.

THE LITERAL SENSE

Thomas says that the literal sense pertains to what the words signify. He says, with regard to the literal sense, "words signify things."[14] This is a bit of shorthand, since, strictly speaking, words signify ideas and those ideas in turn signify things. But "words signify things" gets to the heart of the matter. When considering Scripture literally, the question is: what do the words signify?

This question is the question one asks of any text. The literal sense applies to all books. To read according to the literal sense is to work to understand the signification of the words so as to get at the *sententia* (the idea), and so determine what the author is saying. Thus, all writing has a literal sense. In fact, if it were not for the unique mystical sense of Scripture, one would not even need to speak of its literal sense.

Because the literal sense pertains to what the words signify, the interpreter of the literal sense of Scripture is like any reader of any literary work. "Esau" refers to the brother of Jacob and

---

[14] *ST* I, q. 1, a. 10, resp.

the son of Isaac. That he is a "man" refers to the fact that he is a male of the species, and that he is an "hairy man" signifies a feature of his physical appearance. When Scripture says Abraham has flocks of sheep, it refers to the little wooly creatures that say "baah."

The modern misstep is to equate the literal with the self-evident: when the text is obvious in its meaning, this is a matter of the literal sense. Some passages may be self-evident in their literal meaning, in what the words signify. Abraham signifies the patriarch. But that does not exhaust the literal sense for the simple reason that self-evidence does not exhaust the reading of human literary productions. When St. Paul, quoting Deuteronomy, says, "Our God is a consuming fire,"[15] what does "fire" signify? It is a metaphor, and for the Christian who holds to the immateriality of God, this is obvious. The commentator must ask: for what is it a metaphor?[16] And so the fun can begin. What are the attributes of fire that might be applicable to God and what attributes not? In this the reader of Scripture is no different from the reader of Shakespeare. Sometimes, readers are tentative in their efforts to figure out what the words signify; sometimes, they are simply in the dark. The point is an important one: the difficult work of interpreting the sonnets of Shakespeare is a matter of the literal sense; it can be just as hard making sense of the words of Scripture, but it is still no less a matter of the literal sense. St. Thomas knew the world of classical literary devises as any boy with moderate training

---

[15] Heb 12:29, quoting Deut 4:24.
[16] See *Super Heb* 12:29, lec. 4, Marietti no. 725, for a consideration of the attributes of fire in this passage.

in grammar and rhetoric would. He knew of how poets can use a part for the whole or the whole for a part. He knew of metaphor and irony. He knew of the delights and the tricks of writers. When St. John says that, if all that Jesus said and did were written down, there would not be enough books to contain it, he does not speak falsely; he speaks hyperbolically. It is a figure of speech.[17] All of this is a matter of the literal sense. The commentator who seeks to understand the literal sense of Scripture has serious work to do. Much of Scripture is not particularly clear or obvious in the literal sense. Problems and difficulties and ambiguities arise quickly enough for even casual readers of Scripture. Even when confronted with ambiguous and opaque passages, St. Thomas insists that the literal sense is about what the words signify.

St. Thomas does not say the literal sense is about what the author meant, which might seem a very reasonable understanding of the literal sense, especially when trying to make sense of an ambiguous passage. Thomas does not say that the commentator's task is to figure out and present what the author meant. The closest one might come in Thomas's language to "what the author meant" would be this: the literal sense is concerned with the *sententia*. In this there is a truth, but the student of Aquinas must proceed with caution. Thomas does not speak in these terms; he does not speak of the literal sense as getting at the *sententia*; he speaks rather more mundanely of what the words signify. One might say this is a quibble. After all, the author uses words and he does so precisely so as

---

[17] *Super Heb* 11:32, lec. 7, Marietti no. 628.

to communicate what is in his mind, and so we are clearly in the world of *sententia*. So why does Thomas not speak in these terms? Why does he insist that the literal sense concerns what things are signified by the words instead of what ideas are in the mind of the author?

The answer to this question is found in the practical experience of readers of Scripture (or readers of any text). One finds a splendid example of the problem in St. Augustine's *Confessions*. In the final books of the *Confessions*, Augustine turns from biography to speculative concerns and, in the last two books, to the interpretation of Scripture. Specifically, he turns his attention to the first chapter of Genesis. This is not his first stab at Genesis, nor will it be his last. In the course of his interpretation, he notes that some critics have taken exception to his reading of Genesis. They charge that his interpretation is not what Moses meant. Augustine's reply cuts to the heart of the matter: how do his critics know what Moses meant?[18]

The problem is that Genesis is a notoriously difficult text. Christianity did not have to wait until her modern critics to see it. Christians themselves saw the difficulties (as did the rabbis). Any careful reader could see there were puzzles in Genesis (and if nothing else, the literary and rhetorical training of so many of the Fathers made them careful readers). Augustine gave much of his creative efforts to considering such puzzles, both in the particular (as on Genesis here in the *Confessions*) and in principle (most notably in his *De doctrina Christiana*—On

---

[18] Augustine, *Confessiones*, bk. XII, chs. xiv (17) and xxv (34); for what follows see chs. xiv (17) through xxxii (43). (Note: There are two separate chapter numberings that have been applied to the *Confessiones*, here represented one by Roman numerals and the other by Arabic numerals in parentheses.)

Christian Doctrine). The problem with ambiguous texts is precisely that they are ambiguous. The words are open to multiple possible meanings; or, to use Thomas's language, they are open to multiple possible significations. Augustine's point is that the text is ambiguous. To say that a given interpretation is not what Moses meant is simply not helpful. We return to his question: how do his critics know what Moses meant? They have the same words Augustine does. Short of some new text or a secret decoder ring, the critics have no privileged access to the mind of Moses. They have the same access as Augustine. "What Moses meant" apart from the careful study of the signification of the words is a useless category. And the problem arises precisely from a careful study of the words. A study of the words suggests that Moses could have meant any number of things. The problem is that the words are the access to what the author meant. If the words are ambiguous, puzzling, or opaque, then the access to what the author meant is all the more difficult.

So what is one to do when confronted with an ambiguous passage? How does one get to its meaning? Augustine stakes some claims, and they are all negative. A given interpretation ought not be contrary to reason, contrary to the truths of faith, or contrary to the law of charity. Any interpretation that violates one of these three criteria is necessarily a false interpretation. Augustine is not naive; he knows the criteria themselves are open to debate, as is their application to a given interpretation. Still, they are something. When two competing interpretations present themselves, one can address them according to these criteria, which are at least meatier than "what the author meant."

But what if multiple interpretations of a passage could each be signified by the words and none is in violation of the three criteria? What is one to do then? Augustine's answer is arresting, at least to readers of Scripture formed in a post-Reformation intellectual world. Augustine asks, simply: could not Moses have meant both? Could not all such interpretations of a given passage be true interpretations? And they would be true not only in a narrow sense of fitting the words and criteria but also in a way proper to an authored text: the author meant them. In this case, however, the author meant not simply one thing by his words but many things.

But what if Moses did not mean more than one meaning? What if the reader is confronted with not just two or three alternatives but dozens, maybe hundreds of alternatives. Did Moses mean all of them? Augustine is prepared to entertain the possibility. But he need not insist on it and he does not for the simple reason that Moses is not the only author of Scripture and thus his is not the only meaning in question. God is also the author of Scripture. For the Christian, the more important question is what did God mean when he wrote these words through Moses? Could God have meant more than one meaning? Certainly. Could God have meant hundreds? Certainly. Indeed, it might be particularly fitting that a book that has God as its principal author have such ambiguity. For our purposes, two important points are made by Augustine. First, beware the question of "what the author means" divorced from the signification of the words. When the words themselves are ambiguous, "what the author means" is not a way of resolution. Second, why be concerned with a single meaning?

There is no intrinsic reason why there should be one and only one meaning of a given passage of Scripture. There could be many. Given this, the checks become very important and these checks are the criteria of truth and charity.

This experience of the Fathers, so exemplified by St. Augustine, made medieval thinkers wary of the meaning of the author as a fruitful category of interpretation. St. Thomas knew the critical passages from the *Confessions*; he cites them.[19] And he took their lesson to heart.

Thomas may speak of what the author meant, but it is never by way of argument to determine one reading over another. It is by way of conclusion, not by way of premise. As for the possibility of multiple literal interpretations of a given passage, Thomas's answer in practice seems clear enough: he is thoroughly comfortable with multiple literal interpretations of Scripture. In his most carefully prepared Gospel commentary, the commentary on the Gospel according to St. John, Thomas regularly sets multiple literal interpretations side by side, often drawn from the Fathers. He sets them down and moves on. He rarely adjudicates between them. "This can be explained in many ways without error."[20] Perhaps the most striking instance of this in practice is his *Catena aurea*, his commentary on the four Gospels made up entirely of quotations—*sententiae*—from the Fathers. Here one sees over and over again multiple literal interpretations from the Fathers for a given passage of Scripture. Thomas does not do this so that he can argue against one or show the preferability of one over another. He does it because he holds them all to be true.

---

[19] *ST* I, q. 1, a. 10, resp.
[20] *Super Ioan* 1:3–4, lec. 2, Marietti no. 90.

Thomas, too, addresses the question of criteria for the evaluation of literal interpretations. In his disputed questions *De potentia* (On Power), Thomas asks the question of whether unformed matter was created prior to the creation of things.[21] It is a technical question arising from the meeting of reason and revelation—in this case, Aristotelian philosophy and Genesis. In this regard, it is but one stop in the ongoing discussion from antiquity to our own time of the reading of Genesis, especially the account of the seven days of creation, in relation to what we can know by the investigations of human reason. What makes this question so valuable for our topic is that Thomas here spells out criteria for evaluating multiple literal interpretations of a given passage of Scripture. To do this, Thomas turns to Augustine in the *Confessions* and casts Augustine in his own clear terms. He notes that one can have two areas of dispute. One can dispute the truth of the matter, or one can dispute the meaning of the text (*sensus litterae*). In the disputed question at hand, one can dispute whether in truth there is unformed matter before things, or one can dispute what the words of Genesis mean. These are two different disputes, and for each of them Thomas speaks to what is to be avoided. Like Augustine, his criteria are essentially negative.

With regard to the dispute over the truth of the matter, one should avoid two things. First, one should not assert something false; most especially, one should not assert something contrary to the truth of faith. Thomas has here put together Augustine's truths of reason and truths of faith into a single

---

[21] *De potentia*, q. 4, a. 1, resp., for what follows.

truth, but with a particular warning not to speak against the truths of faith. Second, one should not assert that what one believes to be true is itself a truth of faith. This could prove harmful, for if one's opinion should be shown to be false, it would hold the faith up to the ridicule of non-believers. It is a point with historical merit.

With regard to the dispute over the meaning of the text, here too one should avoid two things. First, one should not attribute something false to Scripture. There can no more be something false in Scripture than there can be something false in the faith, since both are given by the Holy Spirit.[22] Second, one should not so force Scripture to one single meaning (*sensus*) that other meanings are excluded that are also true (i.e., they meet the first criterion) and fit "the circumstance of the letter." What does Thomas mean by the "circumstance of the letter"? He does not say, but the phrase suggests several things. First, a given interpretation needs to fit grammatically and syntactically. Second, a given interpretation needs to make literary sense. If one proposes a metaphor, for example, the metaphor ought to work. And third, a given interpretation should fit the context of the passage in question, what comes before and after it in the text. In practice, one man's circumstance may be well outside another man's pale, but the principle seems clear enough. Should multiple interpretations fit the text and none say something false, one cannot be preferred to the exclusion of the others.

Thus, for Thomas, in considering the literal sense, one must be attentive to the passage itself and its context and one must be

---

[22] It is simply heretical to say that something false is in Sacred Scripture (see *Super Ioan* 12:1, lec. 1, Marietti no. 1730).

attentive to the truth. Such attentions are essential for a sound interpretation. This means that the commentator should have sound human skills in the reading of texts. It also means that the reader should know something of the truth of things.

Having given these principles, Thomas explains why this is the case. It is the peculiar dignity of Scripture that one text may have many meanings, or in his precise language, many senses under one letter.[23] How does this pertain to the dignity of Scripture? First, because in this way Scripture conforms to the diverse intellects of men such that each man may marvel at finding in the passage a truth that he is able to grasp. Second, such multiplicity makes for greater ease in dealing with unbelievers, since, if one's own interpretation is shown to be false, then one can turn to another. With regard to multiple literal interpretations of passages of Scripture, Thomas not only affirms the possibility but further sees such multiplicity as a feature of Scripture's dignity.

In his *Quaestiones quodlibetales* (University Disputations in Answer to Questions posed by others), St. Thomas is asked why God would provide a book with such difficulties in it. Why not make it as clear and self-evident as possible throughout? St. Thomas replies with three reasons. First, such difficulties are useful in fighting boredom, for difficult things give rise to greater attention. Second, difficulty in grasping the truth

---

[23] The context makes clear that he means many literal interpretations of a passage. Nothing in this article is about the mystical senses of Scripture; here Thomas is solely concerned with the question of the literal sense.

removes the occasion of pride. Finally, such difficulty protects Scripture from the ridicule of the unbeliever.[24]

How far St. Thomas is from considering Scripture as being self-evident is seen clearly enough in his frequent practice of adding an explanatory word or two in the text as he quotes the passage of Scripture on which he is commenting. Sometimes he is simply reminding his reader of a pronoun's referent or the subject of a verb. A careful reader might think them obvious, and indeed they are, unless one has lost one's way or simply been distracted at an inopportune moment. At other times, St. Thomas will offer a synonym for a word or a more precise meaning of a particularly capacious term. There is a long tradition of such comments, commonly called "glosses." In the course of the early twelfth century, many glosses on Scripture were formalized in what came to be known as the *Glossa ordinaria*. St. Thomas often refers to "the Gloss" in his writings, and it is, generally, to this work that he refers. Such a practice on the part of so many commentators, including Thomas, reflects a long-standing appreciation of how easy it is to get lost in Scripture. Part of the commentator's task is to make sure even the seemingly obvious is clear; the best commentators realize that no part of Scripture is simply obvious to everyone always.

Finally, we should note the oft-found phrase *quasi dicat* or *ac si dicat* ("as if he were to say"). In his interpretation of a given passage, Thomas will sometimes recast it with *quasi dicat*. In English we might say "in other words." *Quasi dicat* is the simple

---

[24] *Quodlibet* VII, q. 6, a. 1, ad 2. St. Thomas here is yet again following St. Augustine, in this case, his *De doctrina Christiana*.

devise common to many commentators of the Middle Ages who attempt to explain an idea by putting it in other words. It is one more reminder that the words of Scripture require thought and attention to be understood well.

THE MYSTICAL SENSE

We now come to what for moderns is the most incomprehensible aspect of the patristic and medieval reading of Scripture: the mystical sense. To modern sensibilities, the mystical sense is simply the weird sense; the mystical sense is the gateway to the preposterous readings of Scripture that so abound in the Middle Ages.

Thomas is quite clear about what he understands the mystical or spiritual (he calls it either interchangeably) sense of Scripture to be. A correct understanding of the mystical sense hinges upon a correct understanding of the literal sense. Since words signify things, the commentator reads Scripture literally when he works to understand what things the words signify. In considering the mystical sense, the commentator looks to the things signified by the words and works to understand what those things in turn signify. In St. Thomas's succinct phrase, "things signify things";[25] the things signified by the words of Scripture (known in the literal sense) in turn signify other things. This is the stuff of the mystical sense of Scripture.

This distinction between literal and mystical is the foundational distinction in the reading of Scripture. This is so because

---

[25] *ST* I, q. 1, a. 10, resp.

it is founded on the distinction between two kinds of signification: word signifying thing and thing signifying thing.

The things signifying are manifold. They may be plants
(hyssop) or animals (lions). They may be places, like geologi-
cal phenomena (mountains, lakes, rivers), sometimes named
(River Jordan, Mount Horeb), or man-made (the city of
Jericho, the kingdom of Egypt). They may be individual historical figures in a story (Eve, Abraham, Moses). The thing
may be the very story itself (the Passover, the wandering of the
Israelites in the desert for forty years).

St. Paul and St. John provide instances of the mystical sense
in Scripture itself. In his Letter to the Galatians, St. Paul speaks
of Sarah and Hagar as the two covenants.[26] Sarah and Hagar
were not covenants; they were women: one of them the wife of
Abraham and the other the slave of the wife. Both are mothers
of Abraham's children. They are also signs of covenant relationships. How is it that they are such signs? What they are
signs of and how they are signs of it are illuminated by their
relational and social status and circumstances: both are in relation to Abraham, but one is free and one is slave. In this they
signify two covenants. Paul does not say this is a metaphor; he
says it is a mystery and thereby implies something lying deeply
within the course of history.

For his part, St. John reports in his account of Jesus's cru-
cifixion that Pilate sent his men to expedite the death of Jesus
and the two men who had been crucified with him by break-
ing their legs. John says that, since Jesus was already dead, his

---

[26] Gal 4:22–24; *Super Gal* 4:24, lec. 7, Marietti nos. 252–54.

legs were not broken. And then he adds a significant comment that this was all done that the words of Scripture might be fulfilled: "None of its bones shall be broken."[27] The "it" here is the Passover lamb; John refers to the instructions for the preparation of the Passover lamb in Exodus 12:46. There is no prophetic text that says, "when you crucify Jesus, be sure not to break his bones"; nor is there even such an instruction in general with regard to the Messiah. If there were, one would have a fine example of literal prophecy and its fulfillment; the words would signify the thing. Something else is at work here. Jesus's legs were not broken by the Romans because the bones of the Passover lamb were not broken. How are we to understand the passage? For St. Thomas—indeed for all the Middle Ages—it is simple. The words of the Passover story in Exodus refer to Passover. When the Jews are instructed in the preparation of the lamb, the word "lamb" refers to the little woolly mammal that says "baah." That is what the word signifies. The word does not signify Jesus Christ. What signifies Jesus Christ is the Passover lamb itself. In the case of Passover, God's hand and governance are clear and immediate, as are his instructions: no bones to be broken. This is so that the lamb's signification of Christ on the Cross will be clear. It is the lamb itself that signifies, not the words of Exodus. If one has this perspective, then the passage in John's account of the death of Jesus makes sense.

The mystical sense is itself frequently divided further into three senses: the allegorical, the tropological, and the

---

[27] John 19:33, 36; *Super Ioan* 19:36, lec. 5, Marietti no. 2461.

anagogical. These are all instances of the mystical sense, since each looks to what the things that are signified in the literal sense in turn signify. One speaks of the fourfold sense of Scripture, but it would perhaps be truer for St. Thomas to speak of the twofold sense of Scripture, the second of the two itself having a threefold sense. The division of the mystical sense is rather loose. Thomas is not unaware of its history.[28] While the "fourfold" division ultimately won the field, it was not alone in the Middle Ages. One can find threefold schemata; one can find ninefold schemata. Even in cases of numerically identical divisions, the terms may vary in meaning, as not all threefold divisions are exactly the same. What is constant throughout is the initial division of literal or historical from mystical or spiritual. The variety appears on the level of the mystical sense. The question is how many mystical senses there are and how they are to be understood. Thomas stakes a claim but hardly seems doctrinaire about it. He adopts a traditional threefold division: allegorical, tropological, and anagogical. More precisely, he adopts three traditional names. He understands "allegorical" to refer to things that signify Christ, most especially things in the Old Testament that signify Christ. "Tropological" refers to things that signify the moral life in Christ. "Anagogical" refers to things that signify eternal beatitude with Christ.[29]

Thomas himself gives a handy example of the four senses using Genesis 1:3, "Let there be light." "When I say 'Let there be light' and speak of corporeal light, it pertains to the literal sense. If 'Let there be light' is understood as 'let Christ be

---

[28] *ST* I, q. 1, a. 10, ad 2.
[29] *ST* I, q. 1, a. 10, resp.

born in the Church,' it pertains to the allegorical sense. If it is understood as 'let us be introduced into glory through Christ,' it pertains to the anagogical sense. If it is understood as 'let us be illumined in our intellects and inflamed in our affections,' it pertains to the moral sense."[30]

Several points should be made. Not every passage of Scripture admits of interpretation according to all four senses. Except in the one case just quoted in which Thomas is giving an example of the mystical senses, I know of no passage on which he comments by explicitly running through all three mystical senses. Sometimes he will note the specific mystical sense: "This psalm can be explained literally about David; mystically or allegorically about Christ, and morally about the just man and heretics."[31] More often, he will introduce a comment with "mystically" without specifying which of the mystical senses is at work. It is not always easy to tell. I do not think St. Thomas particularly cares. He notes what he sees.

Thomas is famed for his position that the mystical must be founded upon the literal.[32] We can see what that would mean for St. Thomas. If the mystical sense is concerned with things signifying things, then one would want to be as clear as possible about just what those initial signifying things are. One gets to that by being clear as to what the things are that the words of Scripture themselves signify. Thus, the mystical builds on the literal. Thomas may not mean more than this. One must

---

[30] *Super Gal* 4:24, lec. 7, Marietti no. 254.
[31] *In Psalmos* 10:1 (Parma ed., 14:177, no. 1).
[32] *ST* I, q. 1, a. 10, resp.

give careful attention to the literal precisely to get at the thing being signified.

Some distinctions are in order. We need to distinguish between the metaphorical (which is a matter of the literal sense) and the mystical. When St. Paul says, "Our God is a consuming fire," his words do not signify a raging forest fire; they signify divine attributes, and getting at those attributes is a matter of the literal sense, because it is still getting at what the words signify. When the psalmist says Jerusalem is a city built of strong and compact walls, his words signify a real city and real walls. This is the literal sense. Jerusalem itself, the thing, may signify something else, such as the Church or eternal beatitude. Here the commentator will look to the thing itself and its description, such as its strong compact walls, and consider what it signifies about the Church or eternal beatitude. Such interpretation is not a matter of metaphor; it is of a different order.

Likewise, not every moral teaching is to be taken as tropological. The moral teaching of the Decalogue or the Sermon on the Mount can be interpreted literally. Efforts to figure out just what the words of Moses or Jesus signify is the business of the literal sense. When Jesus gives thanks before feeding the five thousand, he gives a moral example, and explaining that is a matter of the literal sense.[33]

Or again, not every teaching on the beatific life with Christ is to be taken as anagogical. The parables of Jesus, for instance, are places for great care in this regard. The metaphorical

---

[33] *Super Ioan* 6:11, lec. 1, Marietti no. 861.

character of the parables does not remove them from the literal sense. When Jesus says, "The kingdom of God is like . . . ," he has not necessarily moved to a mystical sense. The explanation of his parables is first and foremost a matter of the literal sense. Again, we could consider the city of Jerusalem in Revelation. In so far as St. John is describing eternal beatitude as the heavenly Jerusalem, the commentator on Revelation is concerned, at least initially, with the literal signification of the words of St. John. On the other hand, the interpretation of the city of Jerusalem in the Old Testament as the kingdom of heaven is an instance of mystical interpretation, of what the "City of David" signifies.

A danger lurks in the mystical sense, for it would seem to give license to every nut with a loony reading of Scripture. One could make Scripture say anything. To put it perhaps more delicately, but no less pointedly, the mystical senses open wide the possibility, indeed the probability, that readers will simply read into Scripture what they want. Modern readers are, in my experience, generally amused and often appalled at what looks like imagination run amok in patristic and medieval spiritual interpretations of Scripture. This reaction is understandable enough in our own intellectual and religious culture, which is particularly fixed on getting at what an ancient author meant to say in his particular intellectual and religious culture. But the medieval project was not the modern project, and we would do well not to try to make it so. Let us instead ask two questions. First, is there any theological foundation for the mystical senses? Second, are there any checks at all to mystical interpretations?

Is there any theological foundation for all of this? To say that things signify things is certainly clever (something at which medieval thinkers seem to excel); but is it defensible? Can a Christian theological account be given for what they are doing? The answer is yes, and all said and done, the account is rather simple. Things do really signify things. How can they do this? God has so ordained it. God has built these signs into the very fabric of creation and into the very course of history. And because God has so created and governed things, then these signs are, in reality, intrinsic to these things. Precisely because the Christian God is the provident creator and Lord of history, he can do these things. This means that the commentator does not simply make things up and put them in Scripture. He discovers them in Scripture and draws them out. More precisely, Scripture helps him discover things in the very fabric of creation that point to Christ and his saving purpose.

Our second question is: Are there checks? There are certainly no numerical limits. No passage is, in principle, limited to a single allegorical interpretation or a single tropological interpretation. What checks there are will have to be of a different kind. I think, for Thomas at least, one could propose two. First, Thomas says, as has already been noted, the mystical sense is built on the literal sense. This is, indeed, a check on the mystical interpretations but in a particularly interesting way. The literal sense is concerned with the things signified by the words. The mystical is concerned with the things in turn signified by the things of the literal sense. Thus, the soundness of a mystical interpretation will be in proportion to the care with which the commentator has sought to understand the thing signified by the words in the literal sense. The better the grasp of the literal thing, the sounder and deeper the signification of the mystical thing. It is precisely this insight that lies behind the medieval fascination with the physical things of Scripture, such as the properties of plants, the habits of animals, and the movement of the heavens.

Names are a notable instance of this concern. Scripture itself shows a great interest in the meaning of names, both of persons and of places. Medieval commentators, Thomas included, pick this up. The meaning of a name is certainly a concern of the literal interpretation. It can also serve as an indicator for the mystical interpretation. All of these features of things—their properties, their circumstances, their names—are matters for consideration of the literal interpretation. But each of them in turn provides shape and substance to the very thing that itself signifies some other thing. The building of the mystical upon the literal is rather something of an art, an art dependent upon one's understanding the reality of the things signified by the words of Scripture.

As a second check, although he does not say it explicitly, St. Thomas's criteria for the evaluation of literal interpretations could also be used for mystical interpretations. One ought not claim something to be true that is not, nor insist on one's own reading to the exclusion of others. There would be a possible qualification in that the circumstance of the letter might not directly pertain; we could, in the light of what we have just said, say that one ought to preserve the reality of the thing.

Thus we can see there are limits, but they are wide limits indeed, just as the limits on the literal sense are wide. I am inclined to think this is why medieval commentators on Scripture, St. Thomas included, seemed to have so much fun. The playing field is indeed a big one. It has a fence, but the enclosed area is spacious. Or perhaps this might be a better image: Scripture is like a playpen with many splendid toys. It has sides to keep one from falling out and getting hurt, but the area one has is nonetheless a source of fun and joy. I cannot help but think that many of these commentators simply had fun. Of course this was a serious business, but it was about something so huge and capacious that it was itself a source of great delight.

A final note on these various distinctions of senses is called for. The idea is clear enough although not always entirely clear in practice in the tradition or even in St. Thomas. As already mentioned, St. Thomas often enough does not specify which mystical sense he is considering, simply noting "mystically." Sometimes he gives no indication of whether he is reading a passage literally or mystically. He can note a reading is simply "more literal" (*magis literalis)*. The fact is that these are articulated tools to help the commentator, but Scripture is bigger than the categories. The goal is a reading of Scripture that illumines reality in the light of divine truth, not the precise classification of those readings according to the senses of Scripture. The reader of St. Thomas needs to know and understand the senses but (like Thomas) ought not be a slave to them.

Figure

The word "figure" is frequent throughout St. Thomas's commentaries. The Latin term *figura* carries much the same meaning and dimensions as the English word "figure." We speak of a "stick figure," which represents the human form in a few simple straight lines. A "geometrical figure" represents a particular geometrical shape such as a triangle. "Figure skaters" skate in figures such as a "figure 8." The fashion industry speaks of clothing in relation to a person's "figure." Writers use "figures of speech," set forms of speech such as using the whole for the part. Psychologists and literary critics speak of "father figures," which are not actual fathers but like fathers in some way. We apply "figure" to numbers when we say that someone has a "six-figure income" or that the accountant will "run the figures." When we do not understand something, we try to "figure it out." Or we just give up and say, "Go figure." What do all these various uses of "figure" suggest? Figures are figures of something: some kind of likeness of something else, a likeness that gets to a shape or design or pattern that is recognizable and applicable to many things. A figure is a figure of something because it indicates some distinguishing characteristic. It is not the same as the thing itself but points to it. Figure seems to be a particular instance of a sign. This set of interrelated ideas are similarly at work in the Latin *figura*.[34]

For St. Thomas, Scripture is filled with figures. Sometimes, they are a matter of the literal sense. It is the practice of Scripture, St. Thomas says in his commentary on Job, to describe spiritual things by way of corporeal figures. Even though spiritual things are being put forth under the figure of corporeal things, that does not mean that this is a matter of the mystical or spiritual

---

[34] One could consider in a similar way the word "type." Although "type" is common in the Latin tradition when commenting on Scripture, it is not found frequently in St. Thomas's commentaries. He knows it but prefers "figure" and its cognates.

sense of Scripture; this is the literal sense, since this is what the words signify.[35] This use of figure in Scripture is as a literary device.

This is just the beginning. When St. Paul recalls some of the history of the exodus in his first letter to the Corinthians, he directly links the story with Christ, so much so that he says of the rock from which they drank that "the rock was Christ" (1 Cor 10:5). In speaking about this, he says to the Corinthians that "all these things occurred to them by way of figure" (1 Cor 10:11). This is a passage dear to St. Thomas and frequently cited by him. St. Paul says the things of the Old Testament—he says all things—are figures. As "the rock is Christ" would suggest, he saw those things as figures of Christ. For St. Thomas, much of the Old Testament is a figure of Christ as both head and members, which is to say, of both Christ and his Church. This is, in great part, a matter of the spiritual sense of Scripture, of things signifying things.

This runs deeply in St. Thomas's understanding of Scripture. We can see it in his contrasting of figure and truth: a figure is a figure of something, and that something is the truth. Thomas also contrasts truth and falsehood and is very clear that figure is not to be equated with what is false. When Christ contrasts manna with the "true bread" that he gives, St. Thomas asks, was not the manna "true" bread? If one distinguishes true from false, then the manna was indeed true bread; if one distinguishes true from figurative, then the manna is not true bread, but the figure of spiritual bread—the figure of Jesus Christ

---

[35] *Super Iob* 1:6 (Leonine ed., 26:7).

whom the manna signified.[36] What matters is that of which the figure is a figure, that of which it is a sign. The instance here is typical: a corporeal food as a figure of spiritual food.

In this context, St. Thomas says that all of the sacrifices of the Old Testament are figures of Christ and his members.[37] This is why so many practices of the Old Testament were no longer to be followed: that of which they were figures had come. The priesthood of the Old Testament was temporal because it was a figure: it was to pass when he of whom it was a figure had come. In contrast, because Christ is from the truth, his priesthood, like the truth, is eternal.[38] Why is all of this the case? Because of the need for the preparation of souls for faith and the Incarnation. Every miraculous birth of the Old Testament is a figure of the virgin birth of Christ, to prepare souls to believe.[39]

Figures are not found only in the Old Testament. Christ speaks in parables and by way of likenesses, which is to say, in figures. His actions as well as his words can be figures, as in the case of cursing the fig tree.[40]

The Faithful Reader

St. Thomas reads Scripture as a faithful Christian, and he writes for faithful Christians. The Christian's careful reading of Scripture brings him into ever closer and intimate relation to and reflection upon God. The study of Scripture is a matter

---

[36] *Super Ioan* 6:32, lec. 4, Marietti no. 908.
[37] *Super Heb* 13:11, lec. 2, Marietti no. 746.
[38] *Super Heb* 5:6, lec. 1, Marietti no. 252.
[39] *Super Heb* 11:11, lec. 3, Marietti no. 591.
[40] *Super Matt* 21:19, lec. 1, Marietti no. 1713.

of growing in the knowledge of God, or more precisely of the triune God and the incarnate Son. These are truths about God to be known and savored. And why is it so important to know and savor them? Because one cannot love what one does not know. The more one knows of God, the more one can love God.

Dare one say that Thomas reads Scripture as a lover reads letters from his beloved? He reads with affection and care but, perhaps unlike some lovers, without sentimentality. The very attention to detail, the very labor itself, is a manifestation of love, a love that is deepened in the study of Scripture. What is remarkable about St. Thomas is that he expresses it in a thoroughly Scholastic idiom. But even that is not unique. St. Bonaventure and St. Albert worked with much the same intention in the same Scholastic idioms. Even a Scholastic's heart could burn with the love of God and take joy in the reading of Scripture.

CHAPTER 2

THE COMMENTATOR AND THE CAUSES

THE TASK OF THE COMMENTATOR on Sacred Scripture is to help the reader better understand Scripture. That can mean understanding the whole of it or particular parts of it, particular books or passages or words. It is what any good commentator of any book seeks to do.

Such is the case for Thomas Aquinas as a commentator, and he did comment on a number of books, including Sacred Scripture, in the course of his career. St. Thomas is concerned to know the truth of things, to understand reality. The books on which he comments and his commentaries on them are all ordered to this goal. Sacred Scripture has a singular place among the books available to St. Thomas as being the revealed word of God. For St. Thomas as a commentator on Scripture, the study of Scripture is about knowing the truth and communicating that truth to others.

As a commentator, St. Thomas undertakes the task of helping his readers, who are also readers of Scripture, to understand the words of Scripture so as to understand the truths being communicated by those words. Sometimes the words seem clear enough, although there might be more there than first meets the eye. Sometimes the words are not clear; they are ambiguous or puzzling. The commentator's job is to secure the seemingly clear meanings, to explain what may be present beyond what first meets the eye, and to bring clarity and light to what is ambiguous, dark, and unknown. Sometimes a dictionary will suffice for understanding the words, but rarely. The commentator needs to understand the book those words are found in, and in the case of Scripture that means not only the individual book but also that collection of books as a whole which St. Thomas simply calls Scripture.

To achieve such an understanding can be difficult. How to go about doing that? Humans have come up with ways to pursue such understanding, and those ways were grouped in a more or less formal way in the thirteenth century according to "causes." Humans have always done this, more or less systematically, in their efforts to know and understand things more deeply, clearly, and completely. We can see this in the questions we ask in trying to understand things.

When we work to understand things of nature, we ask questions that are reasonable enough. We ask about what is intrinsic to the thing. Children first ask, "What is it?" In answer, we give a name. That name identifies something intrinsic to that thing that makes it what it is, that makes it this particular unified thing—a dog, a cat, a tree. And then, if given half a chance, the child will want to know the parts that constitute that thing, will want to take it apart and see what is inside and figure out how those parts all fit together so as to constitute that thing. In speaking about the what of the thing and the components of the thing, we are asking about what makes this thing to be what it is; we are asking about causes. In this case, the answers are generally known as the "formal" cause and the "material" cause. Children ask yet more questions. At a very early age, the child might ask who made the tree. Or, perhaps a bit more sophisticated, "Where did the dog come from?" Such is the question of "efficient" or "agent" causality. And then there is the question of questions, which can so easily drive parents and teachers to frustration: Why? Why is this dog here? Why are there dogs at all? This is the question of the "final" cause.

The great fourfold division of causes into formal, material, efficient, and final corresponds to four ways of understanding things, four ways in which we ask questions about things, each of which helps us understand that thing better and each of which is needed for a full understanding of that thing.

One can follow the same line of questions for man-made things, such as a table or a painting or a smart phone: Who made it? Why? Out of what? How? And, to get us closer to our task at hand, one can ask these questions about a book. Who wrote it? This is to ask about the efficient cause. Why did he write it? Of course there could be many reasons. A particular subsidiary question would be "what good is it?" or "how is it useful?" This is to look for the final cause, which in the case of man-made things can embrace the question of usefulness. What is it about? This is to look for the material cause. And finally, what is the style or genre of the book? What is the mode of expression? This is to look for the formal cause. This is not a bad set of questions to ask about a book when one wants to understand it since each of the questions could refine one's understanding not only of the whole but of any part of the whole.

Commentators on all kinds of books in the thirteenth century would frequently and explicitly ask these questions at the beginning of their commentaries. St. Thomas will sometimes do so himself at the beginning of his Scripture commentaries. He speaks directly of "the cause of this work" in his commentary on the Psalms.[1] He inquires into the author, matter, mode (form), and usefulness (final cause) of the book of Jeremiah. But Thomas is not particularly fastidious in such analysis. In his commentary on Isaiah, he discusses agent (author), mode, and matter. The consideration of the end (the final cause) is folded into the consideration of mode (formal cause). He does not explicitly address any of the causes in his prologue to his commentary on Job except to say that the author does not really matter. The point here is not the formal exercise at the beginning of a commentary, which can certainly be artificial in itself. The point is that these are broad ways of thinking about things, including books, and that they are an essential part of the way St. Thomas thinks about things. The categories are rich and expansive, and St.

---

[1] *In Psalmos*, prooemium (Parma ed., 14:148).

Thomas uses them with great skill and naturalness through-out his commentaries because he uses them with great skill and naturalness in thinking about everything. They are tools, and this is one of many places where he is not fussy and we need not be fussy either. He does not readily identify causal categories as such in the course of his Scripture commentaries; at best he establishes some valuable general considerations at the beginning of a commentary. But the categories nonethe-less shape his thinking throughout.

St. Thomas would remind us that the causes are all present in created things, which is why they are such valuable tools for understanding things. The goal is understanding things. Each cause contributes to our understanding of the whole thing. Thomas always keeps his eye on the thing. One con-siders the elements—those essential ones pursued by the four causes—but always in the end as ways of better understanding the reality itself. One does not pull a thing apart simply to see what the parts are and then leave them like that; one wants to know what they are precisely to know how they work together when they are in the thing operating as a whole. One distin-guishes in order to unite.

It is perhaps no surprise that St. Thomas, explicitly follow-ing Aristotle, describes wisdom as understanding things in their causes. The truly wise man is the one who understands things in their highest cause, their first principle, which is God. It is the office, the duty, of the wise man to meditate on the principles of things, on their causes, in the light of their first principle, God, and then, in turn, to teach this to others. In the teaching to others, the wise man is both to teach the truth and to refute error.[2] St. Thomas sees this in Scripture: "My mouth shall meditate truth, and my lips hate impiety" (Prov 8:7). This quotation from Proverbs stands at the head of St. Thomas's *Summa contra gentiles*. Such is St. Thomas's understanding of his own life and work. As a reader of Sacred Scripture, St. Thomas seeks to understand things in the light of the highest cause and first principle, which is God. As a commentator on Sacred Scripture, St. Thomas seeks to teach that wisdom to others, precisely as readers of Scripture—so that they too might understand the reality of things ever more profoundly.

---

[2] *SCG* I, ch. 1.

WHY? END OR USEFULNESS
(*FINIS SEU UTILITAS*)

WE BEGIN WITH THE END or usefulness for the simple reason that the final cause is the cause of causes. Children just seem to know this, since their most common question is the question of the final cause: why? We speak here of "end" in the sense of a "goal," not simply in the sense of something stopping or a point of termination. If we know the goal, everything else seems to fall into place. To know the goal is to determine the means: what is needed to achieve that goal or end. The end determines what kind of thing it will be, what it will be made of, even who will make it. When we make something, we must keep our eye on the goal; if we fail in that, we will make something that is not well ordered to that end, or make nothing at all. Likewise, if we want to understand something, we must strive to know its end. The child's driving question is most fittingly, "Why?" That is the question that matters most. If we can understand the why, the end, the goal, then other aspects of the thing will make more sense and we will understand the whole better.

The question of the end can be asked of anything. In the case of man-made things, the question of end can often be asked in terms of usefulness. The question of what it is for is the question of usefulness, of what it is good for. A pen is useful for writing, and indeed we judge its value in relation to its usefulness, in its fulfilling its purpose or end of writing. Books, as works of human art, are no different. If we seek to understand a book, then it would be good to understand its end. What is the goal of the author? And depending on the book, in considering that end, we might well also consider its usefulness. Just what is it good for? With that in mind we could better understand the book; without it, we might well misunderstand it or misconstrue it.

As with anything else, Scripture has an end, a goal. If one is to understand Scripture and then comment on it, one needs to know the end.

The End of Sacred Scripture

When St. Thomas asks in his *Quaestiones quodlibetales* whether there are senses in Scripture other than the literal sense, he begins his response with the end of Scripture. It is a good place to start. "It is to be said that Sacred Scripture is divinely ordered to this, that through it the truth necessary for our salvation should be made known to us."[1] St. Thomas here speaks of truth and salvation. Scripture makes known truth. That truth, however, is ordered to the precise end of the salvation of man. The ultimate end of the salvation of man orders the revealed truth; that is to say, what is revealed is what is necessary for that salvation. As a book, Scripture is communicating something; all those words are signifying something. So, how are we to understand the ideas, the sententiae, of Scripture? They are the truth and a very specific truth: the truth necessary for the salvation of man. Scripture is thus useful insofar as it makes known the truth that man needs to be saved. This governs St. Thomas's understanding of Scripture and thus all his commentary on it.

More can be said. Recall from chapter 2 St. Thomas's description of the usefulness of Scripture in his *De commendatione et partitione Sacrae Scripturae*. He stated that Scripture is more useful than anything else. This is about its end, which is further specified: for all who hold to it come to the life of grace to which Scripture disposes; to the life of justice in works, to which Scripture directs; and finally to the life of glory that Scripture promises and to which it leads.[2] The "salvation" of the quodlibetal question is here stated as "the life of glory." Scripture's usefulness is both in its promise of that life and in its leading to that life. The power of the final cause to give order is manifest. Scripture not only promises and directs to the life of glory but also disposes one to the life of grace and directs one to the life of justice. The life of grace and the life of justice

---

[1] *Quodlibet* VII, q. 6, a. 1, resp.
[2] *De commendatione*, Marietti no. 1202.

matter because they are ordered to the final end of the life of glory. The usefulness of Scripture is ordered and manifold, and this becomes clear when one has the end in sight.

St. John says at the end of his Gospel, "these things were written that you might believe that Jesus Christ is the son of God and believing you might have eternal life in his name" (John 20:31). St. Thomas comments that this pertains to the whole of Scripture, Old and New Testament.[3] The end is that the reader may have eternal life, but for the reader to have eternal life, he must believe that Jesus Christ is the Son of God. This is the truth necessary for salvation made known in Sacred Scripture.

St. Paul writes in his second letter to Timothy: "All divinely inspired scripture is useful for teaching, reproving, correcting, instructing in justice: that the man of God may be perfect, instructed to every good work" (2 Tim 3:16–17). St. Thomas comments that Scripture is useful because it both teaches the truth and exhorts to works of justice that are ordered to the fruit of Scripture, which is to lead man to perfection.[4] St. Thomas's fundamental understanding of Scripture is at work. The end, here beautifully characterized as the fruit of Scripture, is the perfection of man. To bring man to that end, Scripture does two useful things: it teaches the truth and exhorts to works of justice. Scripture is about both what the Christian is to know and also what the Christian is to do. These are useful because, through them, Scripture bears its fruit, which is the perfection of man.

---

[3] *Super Ioan* 20:31, lec. 6, Marietti no. 2568.
[4] *Super 2 Tim* 3:16–17, lec. 3, Marietti nos. 124–28.

Knowing this ultimate purpose is of paramount importance for St. Thomas as a commentator on Scripture. There are, no doubt, many interesting vantage points for the consideration of Scripture: history, literature, sociology, philosophy—the list is potentially a long one. St. Thomas is more than prepared to engage them as a commentator on Scripture. Nonetheless, he always keeps his eye on the prize: salvation. What is in Scripture is there to help man get to eternal life with God. Thomas is remarkable in his ability to keep this focus. There are many aspects of this foundational purpose of Scripture, but in the end, this purpose is determinative. There may be other ways to read Scripture, but they are not Thomas's.

We thus encounter a simple first principle for the reader of Scripture: it is first and foremost about salvation. While individual books each have their own particular focus or purpose, that particular focus is always in the service of the ultimate divine purpose of the whole. In his *De commendatione et partitione Sacrae Scripturae*, Thomas undertakes to give an intelligible ordering to the whole of Sacred Scripture. That order is founded upon the end of Scripture to lead men to the life of glory. Sacred Scripture does this in two ways: by the commandments, which pertains to the Old Testament, and by the gift of grace that the lawgiver bestows, which pertains to the New Testament.[5] The very structure of Scripture as divided into the Old and New Testaments is illuminated by a consideration of the end of the whole.

---

[5] *De commendatione*, Marietti no. 1203.

The End of Specific Books

The question of end can also be asked with regard to each book of Sacred Scripture. Each has its own specific end and usefulness within the ultimate end of bringing man to perfection in the life of glory. Of course there is overlap, and it is more a matter of emphasis than a specific and exclusive usefulness proper to each book. The articulation of an end is a way of trying to understand the book: what it is aiming at. The end guides the commentator both in understanding a given book within the context of Scripture as a whole and in understanding the content of the book itself.

One finds in St. Thomas a splendid array of ends articulated for individual books, but they are always with an eye to the useful truths and exhortations that bear fruit in the ultimate end of eternal life. Let us consider two instances in which St. Thomas speaks directly to the end and usefulness of specific books in his commentaries.

Isaiah

St. Thomas begins the prologues to his commentaries on specific books with a passage from Scripture that illuminates the book and also structures his prologue to it. For his commentary on Isaiah, St. Thomas quotes Habakkuk: "Write down the vision and explain it on tablets so that he who reads it will finish the race because what is seen is still far off but will appear in the end" (Hab 2:2–3). The usefulness of both Isaiah's vision and the prophet's explanation of his vision is expressed in Habakkuk's "so that he who reads it will finish the race." What would it mean to finish the race? To get at this, Thomas begins with three ends: the end of the Law, the end of the precept, and the end of life.[6] What are those ends? The New Testament tells us. "The end of the Law is Christ in justice for all who believe" (Rom 10:4); "The end of the precept is charity" (1 Tim 1:5); and the end of life is death, for "whosoever shall persevere to the end will be saved."[7] We thus have three ends: Christ, charity, and death. Habakkuk says, "so that he who reads it will finish the race," as if to say (*ac si dicat*) that whoever reads without the impediment of doubt will finish the race by believing in Christ, and believing, love and persevere in love.

The usefulness of Isaiah is in the end or goal of being saved. How does Isaiah bring his reader to salvation? First, by belief in Jesus Christ, for the end of the Law is Christ. Isaiah strengthens and informs the faith of the believer so as to read without the impediment of doubt. That believer in turn loves, for the end of the precept is charity. Isaiah calls the believer to persevere in that charity to the very end of this life, for whoever will persevere to the end will be saved. For St. Thomas, Isaiah makes truths of Jesus Christ known by way of prophetic vision. But the usefulness is not simply truths of faith; the usefulness is that, in believing those truths, the believer loves in charity. The fruitfulness of Isaiah is then faith formed in charity persevering to the end. The end is salvation, but here in a specific way ordered to faith, charity, and perseverance. The usefulness is about the end and also about the means ordered to that end. It

---

⁶ For what follows, see *Super Isa*, prol. (Leonine ed., 28:4).

⁷ St. Thomas cites Matt 21, but the editors of the Leonine ed. (vol. 28) surmise that it should be either 24:13 or 10:22.

is about this life—faith, love, perseverance—so as to gain the eternal life that is the ultimate end of all Scripture.

Psalms

St. Thomas's prologue to his commentary on the Psalms begins with a verse from Ecclesiasticus (now more commonly called Sirach): "In all his works, he confessed to him who is holy and exalted in the word of glory" (Sir 47:8).[8] The end of the Psalms, says St. Thomas, is that the soul be joined to God as "to him who is holy and exalted." The Psalms share in the end and usefulness of Sacred Scripture, which is salvation, in the particular way of joining the soul to God. How is this achieved by the Psalms? St. Thomas says, not particularly surprisingly, that the end of the Psalms is prayer; the soul is joined to God in prayer. Prayer is the raising of the mind to God, and St. Thomas describes here four ways in which the soul is lifted up to God: in marveling at the greatness of God's power; in attending to the excellence of God's eternal beatitude; in clinging to the divine goodness and holiness; and in imitating divine justice in deeds. Each of these corresponds to a particular elevation of the soul: marveling at the greatness of God's power is the elevation of faith; attending to the excellence of God's eternal beatitude is the elevation of hope; clinging to the divine goodness and holiness is the elevation of charity; and imitating divine justice in deeds is the elevation of justice.

The end of the Psalms is eternal life characterized as union with God. The means is prayer raising the mind to God. The

---

[8] For what follows, see *In Psalmos*, prooemium (Parma ed., 14:148).

usefulness is seen in how the different ways of lifting one's mind to God foster growth in the virtues that most properly order the Christian's life to the final end of eternal life: faith, hope, charity, and justice. Prayer exercises these virtues, thereby raising the soul to God precisely in and through these virtues. It is hardly surprising that St. Thomas would see in the great prayer book of Sacred Scripture the most important effects of prayer in the human soul: growth in the theological virtues so as to grow in union with God, to progress in that new life begun here so as to come to perfection in eternity.

This does not mean that St. Thomas will explicitly comment on how each psalm lifts up the soul in faith, hope, charity, or justice; that would be tiresome. Rather, he has set a vision for the reading of the psalms such that the faithful reader might see for himself in the particular comments of St. Thomas the ways in which the virtues are exercised in the raising of the soul to God in prayer in that psalm. Attentive praying of the psalms becomes the occasion of the raising of the soul. The psalms are to be prayed, and this would suggest that St. Thomas's commentary is intended to help the Christian reader pray so as to have a heart attentively open to the work of God.

The End and Its Implications

We can see from the examples just given that the end or usefulness of Scripture as a whole or of a particular book is not solely knowledge. The union of man with God is one of intellect and will and ultimately the perfection of the glorified body. Such is eternal life. This orders the means, which are about knowing about matters of faith, but are also about the ordering of the will in hope, charity, and justice (all virtues of the will for St. Thomas). All are necessary for life in this world if it is to be ordered to eternal life in the next—that is, to one's final end.

This guides the Christian commentator. The reader who even casually dips into these commentaries to see what St. Thomas says on a particular passage may be struck by the frequency with which Christ and the Christian life appear in the Old Testament as well as the New. This should not be surprising given the ultimate end of Scripture itself. If the end of Sacred Scripture is the union of man with God and that union is accomplished through Jesus Christ, then the Old Testament has as its goal the union of man with God through Jesus Christ. If that is the goal, if that is precisely Scripture's ultimate usefulness, it sets the contours for the Christian commentator. There may be more or less sophisticated ways of reading these books as Christian books, but such a reading is an inexorable consequence of seeing the end of Scripture as the union of man with God in Jesus Christ. The specificity by book is a specificity, but one already framed by the totality of the providence of God for the salvation of man in Jesus Christ.

Among the implications of this understanding of the end of Scripture is that there can be nothing false in Scripture. If a commentator should propose something false in Scripture, we can be confident that his reading is wrong. We noted in discussing St. Thomas's rules for evaluating an interpretation of Scripture that it cannot be contrary to the truth. We can see one of the reasons for that being so: the end of Scripture as the union of man with God through Jesus Christ. In *De commendatione et partitione Sacrae Scripturae*, St. Thomas spoke of the perfection of Scripture in both the truth and its usefulness. They are distinct but fundamentally related: the usefulness requires that truth, and the immutability of that truth assures its usefulness.

One sees this in St. Thomas's concern for heresy in his commentaries. If Scripture cannot teach error, it certainly cannot teach heresy. St. Thomas considers heresy in two ways in Scripture. We see this consistently in his commentary on the Gospel according to St. John.

There are passages in Scripture that heretics used to support their arguments. St. Thomas acknowledges the heretical use of such passages and comments on how this is a misreading. Given his starting point, even if his own commentary is inadequate as a response to heresy, it does not matter; Scripture cannot teach error. Nonetheless, his task as commentator is to show that such a reading is a twisting of Scripture.

More striking, to me at least, are the passages that St. Thomas reads as working against heresy. St. Thomas has a providential sense of what is found in Scripture as being there precisely to teach the truths of the faith that need to be known so as to counter the heresies that will emerge in the course of time. In his commentary on John, St. Thomas manages to hit all the major Trinitarian and Christological heresies, often multiple times on multiple fronts, to show that Scripture clearly teaches the contrary. Scripture, as the wise man, both teaches the truth and refutes error. On the essential mysteries of the faith—the Trinity and the Incarnation—there is, for the Christian who can see, a fullness of divine teaching to strengthen faith.

End and usefulness also have a place in the mystical inter-pretations of Scripture. Here too one could see criteria for evaluation: whether the interpretation brings the reader into closer union with God. It could be in the particulars of the teaching, or it might just be in the delight of the significa-tion and divine providence. But if it is not useful, what is the point?

Intention of the Author

In commenting on Scripture, Thomas speaks of the "intention of the author." The phrase can cause mischief. Moderns speak of the intention of the author as the meaning of the author. When puzzling over a particularly opaque bit of Scripture, modern scholars will take their task as to get at the intention of the author, what the author meant, so as to illumine what is opaque. This is not what St. Thomas means by intention of the author, and therein lies the opportunity for a misunderstand-ing of St. Thomas.

Thomas has a precise understanding of intention, of which the intention of the author is but a particular instance. "Intention" refers to the final cause of an action as it is in the mind of the agent. More plainly, intention is the answer to the question, "Why did you do that?" Intention is about the end. In the case of writing a book, intention speaks to why the author wrote the book in the first place. The reasons may be many, and the many reasons may be interrelated, some more immediate reasons, some more distant. The key here is that intention pertains to the final cause, the end, the goal.

God, as an author of Scripture, has an intention. That intention is to save man. The particulars of Scripture are all in the service of this overriding purpose. The commentator must know this intention if he is to read Scripture truly and wisely. If he does not understand the ultimate purpose of Scripture—that is, the intention of its divine author—then he is liable to get off track all too quickly, reading it in the light of some other intention.

The human authors of Scripture also have intentions. They must if they are to be true human authors, for all truly human actions require intention. The human authors will have their intentions in writing their books. Insofar as the human authors are contemplative souls, their intentions are, to some degree, the divine intention.

The task of the commentator is to articulate the intentions, human and divine, and there might be any number of ways of articulating those intentions, some more precisely, some more vaguely. Here we see another remarkable feature of the Middle Ages, remarkable at least from the modern point of view. Thomas was hardly the only interpreter of Scripture to articulate the author's intention and to mean by intention the final cause or goal. But not all commentators understand the intention of the author in the same way. One finds differences of emphasis as well as the influence of the interests and concerns of the commentator himself. None of this seems to be of particular concern to the commentators. Authorial intention—both divine and human—seems for Thomas, and for the Middle Ages, to be capacious enough to embrace multiple articulations of intention.

Intention and Ambiguous Passages

The articulation of the intention of the author can be of great help to the commentator confronted with ambiguous passages of Scripture. The commentator is working to understand what the words mean (*sensus*) and what is the idea (*sententia*) being communicated by the author. Getting at the *sententia* is not an easy task. Because *sententia* works principally on the level of ideas, one of the principal aides in figuring it out, especially when the words themselves are ambiguous or difficult, is the intention of the author. Presumably what the authors, human and divine, have to say at any given moment is in the service of their intention, and thus, by knowing their intention, one might be able to see more clearly what the *sententia* of a given passage is. Nonetheless, the essential work remains the signification of the words.

◆

The wise man seeks to know things according to their proper causes, and the truly wise man according to the highest causes. For St. Thomas, the wise man does this for a purpose; the wise man has an end. That end is to judge and order things rightly.[9] If one is to judge and order rightly, one must understand that which is being judged and ordered, and that is a matter of knowing the causes of what is being judged and ordered. Those are best known when known according to their highest and principal causes. The wise commentator on Scripture will be

---

[9] *ST* II-II, q. 45, a. 1.

able to judge and order according to the proper and the highest causes. He must make sense of the words; he must understand, which is to say, make judgments about the meaning of the words of Scripture. To understand the final cause will make his judging and ordering the elements of Scripture that much truer.

The man who is simply wise, wise with regard to all of life, must not only know the highest causes but also judge and order all things in his life according to those highest causes. Scripture, with regard to its goals and its usefulness, is ordered to helping men be wise so as to order their lives more fittingly to their proper end. The faithful reader of Scripture will himself grow in wisdom when he not only sees the end and the means to the end that are being taught but learns from them and reads Scripture in their light. The task of the wise commentator is to help his reader grow in wisdom in the very reading of Scripture.

CHAPTER 4

WHO? AUTHOR
(*ACTOR SEU AUCTOR*)

WHO MADE THESE BOOKS? This is the question of the efficient or agent cause. St. Thomas speaks of the *actor* or *agens* (the one who does something) or the *auctor* (the author, another way of saying the one who does something). This is the question of the authorship of Scripture. St. Thomas's language is not exactly that of moderns, even though the word *auctor* might suggest it. St. Thomas speaks of books being *produced*, not written. The Latin is *editus*, from which we get the English "edit" and "editor." Editors very concretely brings books into existence by their editing. The senior folk at publishing houses are the "editors." The authors are *auctores* or *actores* who do something, and what they do is produce a literary work.

For St. Thomas, Scripture has both divine and human authors. Just how does Thomas understand this twofold authorship? How does this twofold causality help the commentator better understand Scripture? To that we now turn.

The Divine Author

Thomas claims, as Christians do, that God is the author of Sacred Scripture. How to think about that divine authorship? St. Thomas's prologue to his commentary on Lamentations can help us. He begins with a verse from Ezekiel: "Behold a hand was sent to me in which there was a closed book. And it opened the book before me which was written both within and without, and there were written in it lamentations and song and woes" (Ezek 2:9). From this verse, St. Thomas has much to say about the divine authorship of Lamentations.[1] He begins with the divine attribute of kindness, for Ezekiel says, "behold a hand was sent." The connection is not obvious and it takes some spelling out on St. Thomas's part. This hand is the wisdom of God. It is the wisdom by which all things have been made: "You have made all things in wisdom" (Ps 103:24).[2] It is the wisdom that opens the intellect to seeing: "The hand of the Lord is upon me and has led me there to the visions of God" (Ezek 40:1–2). It is the wisdom that prepares the tongue for speaking: "He sent his hand and touched my mouth and the Lord said to me, 'Behold, I have placed my words in your mouth'" (Jer 1:9). It is the wisdom that directs the hand to write: "Fingers appeared

---

[1] For what follows, see *In Thren*, prooemium (Parma ed., 14:668).
[2] The explicit reference to the divine hand is in the following verses. St. Thomas presumes his reader will know the psalm well enough to make the connection.

as of a hand writing" (Dan 5:5). Those fingers are the prophets and other teachers among whom the gifts of wisdom are divided. St. Thomas lays out here an ordered consideration of divine wisdom: it is the very wisdom that has created all things; it is the source of truth; it is the source and surety of that truth in speech and writing in those teachers whom God has sent to hand on the wisdom they have received. It is an exquisitely concise expression of the unfolding of creation and providence as the work of divine wisdom. Each dimension of wisdom arises from the figure of a hand as expressed in Scripture itself.

The hand in the verse of Ezekiel that begins the prologue "was sent." What does that mean? The divine wisdom is so high that, since we are so low, we are unable to receive any of it unless it be sent to us. "Oh, the heights of the riches of the wisdom and knowledge of God!" (Rom 11:33). Here at last we find the kindness of the divine author with which Thomas began his prologue: "The creator can be seen from the magnitude of beauty and the creature" (Wis 13:5). Wisdom is also sent in internal inspiration. "Wisdom moves herself through the nations and into holy souls establishing them as friends of God and prophets" (Wis 7:27). Preeminently, wisdom was sent in the Incarnation when invisible wisdom appeared before our fleshly eyes. "Send her [wisdom] from your holy heaven that she might be with me and labor with me that I might know what is acceptable before you for all time" (Wis 9:10). The kindness of God is found in the communication of divine wisdom to lowly man: in the things of creation to be considered by the human mind, in divine inspiration, and in the Incarnation of the Son of God.

For St. Thomas, divine wisdom is one, and it is a manifestation of God's goodness that his wisdom is communicated in so many ways. Thus Scripture is situated wholly within the communication of divine wisdom in creation and providence. Such a unity of wisdom is the basis of the spiritual senses of Scripture: the wisdom that is the author of Scripture is the same wisdom that created all things and is able to invest them with their own intrinsic signification.

Likewise the wisdom that is the internal inspiration of prophets and teachers, of those who hand on that which they have learned, is the wisdom that is the author of Scripture. The refraction of that wisdom through many prophets and teachers expresses a singular wisdom in multiple human instruments. In this is not only the truth of Scripture but also the unity of Scripture, a unity grounded in the unity of divine wisdom.

Finally and most importantly—preeminently—that wisdom is incarnate in Jesus Christ. Thus all the wisdom in creation and providence, in the particular inspirations of all the authors of Scripture and all teachers, is most fully expressed in Christ, who is that wisdom. It is not only not surprising but positively necessary that all the wisdom of Scripture should point to Christ and that all of Scripture is ultimately read in the light of Christ. Christ is the norm of all things because he is the divine wisdom according to which all things were made.

How fitting this is to the consideration of the end and usefulness of Scripture: to bring man to eternal life. It is not simply that God is the author, but God *as wisdom* is the author: he who has rightly ordered all things is the author. Thus all things, including creation, are ultimately and most perfectly ordered to the eternal life of man. The wisdom of God is such that Scripture is part of that ordering with its own proper place in creation and the unfolding of salvation in the Old Testament and its culmination in the Incarnation.

In this context, we should note that St. Thomas sometimes says that the Holy Spirit is the author of Scripture.[3] In so doing, St. Thomas clearly situates the divine authorship as part of the mission of the Holy Spirit in the salvation of man.

The Human Author

God is the author of Scripture. He is, in the language of St. Thomas, the efficient cause, the agent cause. Men, too, are authors of Scripture. They, too, are the efficient cause. How do these two efficient causes, these two agents or authors, stand in relation one to another? The human authors are God's instruments; they are what St. Thomas calls "instrumental" causes.[4] The reader of St. Thomas must exercise some caution here. "Instrument" sounds so insignificant. Even worse, it may call to mind a bored and distracted court stenographer.

Let us be clear about instrumental causes. An instrumental cause is a real cause; it truly brings something about. My ever-at-hand fountain pen is a real cause, albeit instrumental, to the writing of a letter to my wife. I could, of course, write her a letter by some other means, such as a different pen (the cheap plastic one in the hotel) or a pencil, or I could dispense with

---

[3] See, e.g.: *ST* I, q. 1, a. 10, resp.; *Quodlibet* VII, q. 6, a. 1, ad 5 (the principal author of Sacred Scripture is the Holy Spirit); *In Psalmos*, prooemium (Parma ed., 14:149), and *Super Isa*, prol. (Leonine ed., 28:3).

[4] See, e.g., *Quodlibet* VII, q. 6, a. 1, ad 5, in which St. Thomas says the principal author of Sacred Scripture is the Holy Spirit, and man is an instrumental cause.

paper entirely and simply send her a text. To achieve my goal of writing to my wife, a number of means, or instruments, are available to me. Once, however, I have actually written it, the now real and existing letter has, as an equally real cause, not only me as the writer but my fountain pen.

So it is with Scripture. God writes with men. The men who are the authors of Scripture are real causes of Scripture. They actually wrote it. They are, in relation to God, real causes, but instruments, rather like my fountain pen. Could God have produced Scripture otherwise? Certainly. He could have chosen other men (as I could use a different pen). He could have circumvented men entirely and simply produced Scripture himself and dropped it out of the sky (rather what I understand texting to be). Thus, while God might have achieved the production of Scripture any number of ways, the Scripture he did produce, the Scripture we have before us, has, as a real cause, the men who authored the books. Instrumental causes may be in the service of a primary cause, but they are no less real causes for that fact. So it is with the human authors of Scripture.

An instrumental cause is more or less well suited to the task to be done. I vaguely recall an advertisement of some years ago that asked: "Ever try to write with a banana?" I suppose the ad was for some brand of pen. The point is obvious enough: a banana may look at first glance like something to write with, but it is not well suited to the task. I could imagine that there have been people desperate to write who, with only a banana at hand, did indeed try to write with it, even with some success. But I would think those people would happily give up the banana when offered a pen. Even among instruments made for the task, some are better suited to it than others. This is why some of us carry a fountain pen—it is better suited to the task of writing than the cheap hotel ballpoint pen.

Such is also the case with Scripture. God writes with men, and he does so because they are suitable instruments. Being suitable instruments can be taken in two ways. First, it is suitable that there be an instrument and that that instrument be a man. It is fitting that, if God speaks to men, he speak through men. If such is the case in the fullest instance of revelation, the Incarnation, it should be so also in the case of Scripture. Second, one could speak of the individual authors as suitable not simply in their species but in their persons.

This comes into focus if we consider how St. Thomas speaks of some specific human authors.

Isaiah

We recall that for his commentary on Isaiah St. Thomas quotes Habakkuk 2:2–3 at the beginning of his prologue: "Write down the vision and explain it on tablets so that he who reads it will finish the race because what is seen is still far off but will appear in the end."[5] St. Thomas finds three points in the passage from Habakkuk about the author: the author, the minister of the author, and the office or gift of the minister.

The author is found in the command of the one speaking. Habakkuk introduces the passage just quoted saying, "The Lord responded to me and said..." This author, the one who commands, is the Holy Spirit. If the Holy Spirit is the author,

---

[5] For what follows, see *Super Isa*, prol. (Leonine ed., 28:4).

the prophet is the minister of the author, and he is expressed in the passage from Habakkuk in the act of the one writing. The command is "write!" And that is what the minister does. "The tongue of the prophet is the instrument of the Holy Spirit, as is said in the Psalm, 'my tongue is the pen of the swiftly writing scribe'" (quoting Ps 44:2). The relationship of the Holy Spirit to the prophet is that of agent to his instrument. That instrument is called a "minister" (*minister*). A minister is a subordinate, a servant, but the stress is on assistance, on the task to be done, the duty to be fulfilled. St. Thomas could have used "servant" or "slave" (*servus*), but he chose not to because he wanted to emphasize the personal agency, the causality, of that human instrument of the minister. The minister, the instrument of the author, is himself an agent. He does something: he speaks and writes.

In addition to the author and the minister is the office or gift of the minister. "Office" (*officium*) pertains to a formal duty or responsibility; in this instance, it is an office that is also a gift. That office, that gift, is "the privilege of vision." That it is a privilege means that it pertains to the person. It is expressed in Habakkuk in "the vision" that the prophet is to write down. St. Thomas yokes prophecy with vision because Scripture does. "Who is today called a 'prophet' was at one time called 'him who sees'" (quoting 1 Kgs 9:9). Through the privilege of vision, the prophet is the minister of the Holy Spirit. He is no unthinking slave; rather, he is a fitting human instrument prepared uniquely by God to serve as a human author of Sacred Scripture.

What St. Thomas says of the prophet in his prologue to his commentary on Isaiah is true not only of Isaiah, but of any prophet. That he highlights these particular elements of prophecy indicates what he thinks is particularly characteristic of Isaiah as a prophet. For St. Thomas, Isaiah's office is especially marked by vision. As such, it will inform St. Thomas's reading of Isaiah and his commentary on it.

Jeremiah

We can appreciate how St. Thomas's emphases in considering the office of the prophet shape his understanding of a given prophet if we consider the prologue to his commentary on Jeremiah in contrast to the prologue to his commentary on Isaiah. He begins the prologue with a quotation about Jeremiah from 2 Maccabees: "This is the lover of his brothers and the people of Israel; this is he who prays much for the people and for the entire holy city, Jeremiah the prophet of God" (2 Macc 15:14). From this passage, we learn three things about the human author: his office, his affection, and his action.[6]

"Jeremiah, the prophet of God." This is his prophetic dignity, which is his office, and it stands in direct relation to God. St. Thomas contrasts the "prophet of God" with "prophets of the heavens" and "prophets of the devil." Prophets of God receive divine illumination about future things through the mediation of angels. Prophets of the heavens are astrologers and more generally all those who practice any kind of divination from the observation of nature so as to conjecture about the future. Prophets of the devil know something that will happen in the future from the revelation of demons. The

---

[6] For what follows, see *In Jer*, prooemium (Parma ed., 14:577–78).

prophecy of the prophets of God is a proclamation of the unfolding of future events marked by immutable truth illuminating the way to eternal glory. The prophecy of the prophets of the heavens lacks immutable truth because it proclaims contingent effects of proximate causes and not necessary effects from first causes; it is bogus and illuminates nothing. The prophecy of the prophets of the devil is more dangerous. It might well have truth, given the demons' keen grasp of causality, but because it is demonic, such prophecy is deceptive and ordered to the harm of man. These prophecies, even if they truly proclaim future events, do not illuminate man's way to eternal glory, but draw him away from it. The prophet of God alone holds a true office in relation to God's divine authorship because the prophet of God alone has knowledge truly ordered to the end of eternal glory. St. Thomas exquisitely uses the final cause of Scripture to distinguish the true instrument.

St. Thomas then turns to the affection of the human author: what are the loves that move the prophet? The passage from 2 Maccabees that heads the prologue describes Jeremiah as a lover of his brothers. Such are the prophets of God. St. Thomas quotes the final chapter of the letter to the Hebrews: "May the charity of fraternity remain in you and may you not forget hospitality" (Heb 13:1–2). What is that charity of fraternity? To instruct with true teachings, as God says in Jeremiah: "I will give you shepherds after my own heart and they shall feed you with knowledge and teaching" (Jer 3:15). The affection is thus united with the office and its proclamation of the immutable truths that illuminate man's way to eternal glory. That proclamation is an expression of the prophet's love for his brothers.

Finally, there is the action of the human author. In the words of 2 Maccabees, Jeremiah "prays much for the people and for all the holy city." The action is prayer and in that action is shown his pious compassion for his people. St. Thomas says the greatness of his prayer is in the height of his contemplation, in the great magnitude of his compassion, and in his constancy over time both before and after the Babylonian captivity.

St. Thomas brings these three elements together. The prophet requires the prophetic dignity, the fraternal charity, and the piety of compassion because the prophet stands between God and the people. Thomas quotes Moses speaking to the people: "I was a mediator between God and you" (Deut 5:3). Therefore, he concludes, the prophet must be joined to God through the gift of prophecy (office) and to the people by the chain of charity (affection), and by his prayers bring the cause of the people to God and by his preaching bring the cause of God to the people (action).

As he had in the prologue to his commentary on Isaiah, St. Thomas articulates the attributes of the prophet. He does not mention Jeremiah by name but speaks simply of "the prophet," and the essentials he describes would fit any prophet. And yet he has his eye specifically on Jeremiah, as we can see in the reference to his constancy during the time of the Babylonian captivity. As St. Thomas stressed vision in introducing Isaiah, so he stresses mediation in introducing Jeremiah, signaling a theme in his own understanding of Jeremiah and a theme marking his own commentary. Here, too, St. Thomas shows how Jeremiah is a uniquely fitting instrument as a human author of Scripture.

St. John

What is most significant about St. John is not that he was one of Christ's apostles or even that he was the beloved disciple. What is most significant is that he was a contemplative. St. Thomas heads the prologue of his commentary on St. John's Gospel with a verse from Isaiah: "I saw the Lord sitting on a high and lofty throne, and all the earth was filled with his majesty, and what was beneath him filled the temple" (Isa 6:1). Using these words, Thomas provides a beautiful and succinct summary of the contemplation of the incarnate Word and then shows how St. John most perfectly exemplifies the sublimity, fullness, and perfection of such contemplation. The sublimity of the contemplation is the contemplation of God in which the eye is lifted above all created things. "Because John transcended all created things, the very mountains, heavens and angels, and came to the Creator himself of all things, it is manifest, as Augustine says, that John's contemplation was the highest."[7] The fullness of contemplation is the contemplation not only of the essence of God but also of the power and effects of God as they extend to all things. Here too St. John was lifted up to the contemplation of the nature and essence of the divine Word and its power extending to all things.[8] The very perfection of contemplation occurs when the contemplative is raised to the heights of the incarnate Word and adheres to it in love as its end. St. John was raised to this perfect contemplation in love.[9] Why does this matter

---

[7] *Super Ioan*, prol., Marietti no. 2.
[8] *Super Ioan*, prol., Marietti no. 7.
[9] *Super Ioan*, prol., Marietti no. 8.

to St. Thomas? It says something essential not simply about St. John the apostle but about St. John the evangelist. It says something about what kind of an instrument he was. As a contemplative, John knew of what he spoke in writing his Gospel. He knew not simply the history he reports, but he knew the divine reality he was communicating. John writes as a true human author, as one who writes what he knows. John knows what he writes because he is a contemplative. That is the most authentically human way he could know those things. Because John is the beloved disciple and because that beloved disciple is a contemplative soul, he is a most fitting instrument to communicate what God would have him communicate precisely because he knows the reality he is to write about.

The human author is a graced instrument. That grace is like all grace according to St. Thomas: it perfects the human person. As a contemplative raised to the heights of the incarnate Word, St. John is more perfectly St. John, and thus his Gospel thoroughly reflects him. Grace is needed, and a particular grace that makes the evangelist sensitive to the movement of the Holy Spirit, but that movement is one that is wholly consonant with the reality that is St. John. Christ says to his apostles: "The Holy Spirit, whom the Father will send in my name, he will teach you all things, and call to mind for you all things, whatever I have said to you" (John 14:26). St. Thomas indicates the value of this promise: "For it is to be known that, of those things that Christ said to his disciples, some they did not understand and others they forgot. Therefore the Lord says, 'He will teach you all things' that you do not now understand, 'and will call to mind for you all things' that you could not commit to memory." And then he applies it to St. John the evangelist, who according to tradition wrote his Gospel late in the first century. "For how, after forty years, could John the evangelist remember all the words of Christ that he wrote in his Gospel, unless the Holy Spirit had called them to his mind?"[10]

St. Paul

For St. Thomas Aquinas, as for the whole of the Middle Ages, St. Paul is simply "the Apostle." This supernatural reality is defining and shapes St. Thomas's presentation of St. Paul as human author. He begins his general prologue to his commentary on the letters of St. Paul with the words of Jesus explaining to Ananias in Damascus why he should go to the blinded Paul: "This man is my chosen vessel to carry my name to nations and kings and the children of Israel" (Act 9:15).[11]

In an extended and refined meditation on vessels, St. Thomas explains what it means for St. Paul to be Christ's chosen vessel, a vessel of wisdom and charity, decorated, as it were, with all the virtues. All of this renders him a useful vessel. Useful for what? To be an apostle of Jesus Christ. Christ has made St. Paul his vessel and has made him precisely the vessel he needs so as to be filled with that particular abundance of graces that constitutes the bearing of the name of Christ. For St. Thomas, St. Paul is an apostle not simply because he knows something about Christ, but because his life is conformed to

---

[10] *Super Ioan* 14:26, lec. 6, Marietti no. 1960.
[11] For what follows, see *Super epistolas s. Pauli*, prol., Marietti, nos. 1–10.

Christ in his knowing, in his loving, in the entirety of his life. St. Paul himself says: "It is not I who live, but Christ who lives in me" (Gal 2:20).[12] This is what it means to bear the name of Christ.

For St. Thomas, St. Paul's life, as St. John's, is marked by holiness, but it is not generic holiness. In each, Christ shapes his instrument. For St. John, it is a matter of contemplative heights and a fullness of wisdom. For St. Paul, it is a holiness ordered to the active life of the man who would simply be known as "the Apostle," the vessel intended in a particular and unique way to carry the name of Christ.

While we might be surprised that St. Thomas's presentations of Isaiah, Jeremiah, St. John, and St. Paul as authors have little to say about their historical circumstances, St. Thomas is nonetheless interested in their uniqueness as authors. Each is shaped to be who he is in relation to God so as to communicate most personally and most perfectly what he has been given. Each stands as an exquisite instrument, fully human and as such ordered to the end of human life that is the end of Scripture itself.

Holy Commentators

In his prologue to his commentary on Lamentations, St. Thomas says that the mysteries of Sacred Scripture require explanation.[13] They require *expositio*, an opening up, a making known, an explanation. That work is done by

---

[12] *Super epistolas s. Pauli*, prol., Marietti no. 3.
[13] For what follows, see *In Thren*, prooemium (Parma ed., 14:668).

commentators—that is, *expositores*—who open up Scripture, who make known and explain its mysteries. These are not just any commentators, these are holy commentators (*sacri expositores*), for, St. Thomas says, the Scripture is explained (*exposita*) by the same Spirit by which it was produced. Scripture requires explanation, and that explanation is the work of the Holy Spirit who is its principal author. The work of the Spirit with regard to Scripture continues beyond the authors of Scripture to the holy commentators. The way of operation is the same: the presence of the Holy Spirit in the life of grace. The commentators who matter are the holy commentators. Their holiness is precisely the mark of their being instruments of the Holy Spirit.

Who are these holy commentators? St. Thomas would certainly not count himself among them. He speaks of the holy teachers (*doctores*), first and foremost, those figures we call the Fathers of the Church. When St. Thomas speaks of "fathers" (*patres*) he does not mean early Christians; he means the fathers of the Old Testament, those figures we call the patriarchs. For St. Thomas, the "teachers" are those who have explained the faith; those teachers who did so commenting on Scripture are "commentators." What matters first and foremost for St. Thomas is their holiness; he speaks of holy teachers and holy commentators.

Among the holy teachers, there is an ordering. If we are to understand St. Thomas's commentaries, we must understand this hierarchy among commentators. In speaking of holy teachers, St. Thomas distinguishes the prophets and apostles (those teachers who are the authors of Sacred Scripture) from the other teachers (those teachers who come after the apostles).[14] The distinction matters because it is a distinction of authority. The authority of the prophets and apostles is both intrinsic and necessary to the science of sacred doctrine, to the study of sacred teaching. When he says it is intrinsic, he means that their authority is proper to sacred teaching and not to some other branch of human knowledge and inquiry (such as physics). When he says it is necessary, he means that their authority is such that their teaching is necessarily true: it is to be assented to with certitude. This follows from divine authorship and God's revelation of immutable truth.

St. Thomas distinguishes the authority of the prophets and apostles from the authority of the other holy teachers. The authority of the other holy teachers is intrinsic but *probable.* The prophets and apostles command assent because their teaching is necessarily true; the other holy teachers do not because their claim is one of probability. We might say we give the latter the benefit of the doubt. The fact that St. Augustine said something does not guarantee its truth; but one ought to take it seriously and be slow to contradict. Their holiness establishes their relationship with God so as to be fitting instruments in his service, as with the authors of Scripture itself. But in the case of the holy teachers, their holiness does not guarantee the truth of their teachings, although it does make it probable.

Insofar as the holy teachers wrote commentaries on Scripture, they are holy commentators, with all their attendant authority. As such, they have a prominent place in the

____

[14] For what follows, see *ST* I, q. 1, a. 8, ad 2.

commentaries of St. Thomas; in fact, they are present throughout St. Thomas's commentaries. He cites them frequently. He was eager to learn from them. There is a story in the early biographies of St. Thomas that, when he was returning to Paris, the confrère accompanying him remarked on the great beauty of the city, to which St. Thomas responded that he would happily give the city of Paris for St. John Chrysostom's commentary on St. Matthew. This is no slight on thirteenth-century Paris; it is a tribute to the place of St. John Chrysostom in the mind of St. Thomas.

St. Thomas's commitment to the holy commentators is seen dramatically in his *Catena aurea* on the Gospels. There are no words of St. Thomas in the *Catena*. The *Catena* is a collection of comments of the holy teachers on the whole of the Gospels. St. Thomas has culled essential thoughts—*sententiae*—of the commentators to expound the Gospels. He says that he has taken the liberty of editing passages but that he has worked to preserve the meaning. Modern editions indicate the source in the body of the text. This is annoying. St. Thomas noted the sources in the margin; the text is to be read as a flowing, running commentary constructed of the words of the holy teachers. It is an intellectual and literary achievement of the first order. That he could produce such a work tells us of the great care with which St. Thomas studied and indeed mastered the holy teachers. And it also tells us that his devotion to them is typical of the Middle Ages, for the *Catena aurea* was among the most popular of St. Thomas's writings.

Within his own commentaries, the holy teachers have pride of place. Given the possibility of multiple literal explanations of Scripture, St. Thomas has no problem setting explanations of the holy teachers next to each other without comment in his own commentaries. They rarely—if ever—truly contradict each other, but they do offer different explanations, and they fit the criteria for evaluating an explanation. And they are the holy teachers and worthy of the benefit of the doubt. As St. Thomas says in the prologue to Lamentations, they, too, are guided by the Holy Spirit. That does not mean that St. Thomas would never disagree. He does.[15] Nor does it mean that he might not prefer the reading of one teacher over the reading of another. He does.[16]

For the modern reader who prizes originality and personal distinctiveness, the commentators clutter St. Thomas's commentaries and the *Catena aurea* was the colossal waste of time of a great mind. But unlike the modern reader, St. Thomas did not prize originality. He prized the truth and understood that the holy teachers held a special place in communicating the truth, marked as they were by great intelligence informed by holiness. If one wants to know the mind of St. Thomas—and not simply the novel ideas of St. Thomas—one needs to be especially attentive to the holy teachers in his writings. They are not there simply to provide authority for what he happens to think anyway. They are there to state the truth that, because of their authority, Thomas himself holds.

Not all of the figures of the past that Thomas cites are holy teachers. He cites Origin with respect, fully aware that he held

---

[15] See. e.g., *Super Ioan* 13:1, lec. 1, Marietti no. 1738, rejecting a reading of St. Augustine as simply false.

[16] See, e.g., *Super Ioan* 18:24, lec. 4, Marietti no. 2325, preferring a reading of St. Augustine over a reading of St. John Chrysostom.

positions later condemned as heresy. He too is a valued commentator on Scripture, most likely because the Church so values him, even with a caveat in doctrinal matters.

The holy commentators on Sacred Scripture extend the work of the Holy Spirit and thus merit a special place in the faithful reading of Scripture. St. Thomas understands his role as a commentator to help his readers understand Scripture as the holy commentators understood it for the arresting reason that this is how the Holy Spirit guided the interpretation of what the Spirit wrote in the first place.

There are the teachers who are the authors of Scripture, the prophets and apostles; then there are the other holy teachers. Then there is everyone else, among whom St. Thomas would count himself. This helps us understand the common thirteenth-century practice of not naming contemporary authorities for the simple reason that contemporaries were not authorities. In sacred teaching, the holy teachers are the authorities and named as such. St. Augustine could and should be named. The holy teachers extend at least to St. Bernard in the century before St. Thomas. Contemporaries, however, were not to be named but simply referred to as "some say." Such a practice is particularly frustrating for the modern scholar, but it speaks clearly to how St. Thomas and his contemporaries understood the place of their work in sacred teaching.

St. Thomas's explicit and articulated relationship with the holy teachers exemplifies his understanding of his work as part of the Church. There are other ways to read Scripture, but St. Thomas is not especially interested. What matters to him is precisely the place of Sacred Scripture in holy teaching as a place of truth, a truth secured, protected, and expounded in the Church.

The Church in her worship provides guidance to the reader of Scripture. St. Thomas says that the principal subject matter of Isaiah is the appearance of the Son of God. On what does he base this? Isaiah is read during Advent.[17] Jeremiah on the other hand is principally about the mystery of the Passion. On what does he base this? Jeremiah is read during Passiontide.[18] To think about Isaiah and Jeremiah is to think about how they are read in the life of worship of the Church.

Or again, in his commentary on the Gospel of St. Matthew, St. Thomas addresses the question of how long Christ preached; that is, how long is the time between his baptism and his Passion.[19] St. Thomas notes two opinions. Some say it was two and a half years, and according to them, the miracle at the wedding feast at Cana took place the same year as Christ's baptism. Thomas prefers a longer period of preaching on the grounds of the mind and custom of the Church, by which he means the liturgy. The feast of the Epiphany commemorates three events: the adoration of the Magi, the baptism of Christ occurring on the same day thirty years later, and the miracle of the conversion of water into wine at Cana occurring on the same day the following year. The presumption of each event occurring on the same day arising from the practice of the Church guides Thomas's thinking with regard to the historical question of the length of Christ's ministry.

---

17 *Super Isa*, prol. (Leonine ed., 28:4); see also *De commendatione*, Marietti no. 1207.
18 *De commendatione*, Marietti no. 1207.
19 *Super Matt* 4:12, lec. 2, Marietti no. 349.

◆

The authorship of Sacred Scripture for St. Thomas is a unity of God and man. God is the principal author; men are instruments. The human instruments are instruments precisely because they are informed by the same Holy Spirit that is the principal author; they are formed in being united to God in contemplative holiness. The perfecting movement of the Holy Spirit renders each author uniquely himself and in so doing renders him a most fitting instrument. Scripture unfolds providentially and particularly in the lives of its human authors. The significance of Sacred Scripture in its end of the salvation of man means that, for St. Thomas, the Holy Spirit not only guides the authors of Scripture but also guides the Church in her holy teachers and commentators to communicate the saving wisdom of Scripture over time. As a commentator, St. Thomas understands his task as a participation in the communication of this salvific divine wisdom.

CHAPTER 5

WHAT? MATTER
(*MATERIA*)

Matter

The foundational instance of matter is the body of an animal. The body is a whole made up of parts (organs, blood, cells). All of these elements pertain to the matter of the animal, and all are the object of study of the biologist. Generally speaking, it is good for the biologist to have a sense of the whole so as to understand how the various parts contribute to the whole.

When we apply this to a book, we ask, "What is the book about?" This is what St. Thomas calls the "matter" of the book or what we might now call the "subject matter." The matter of a book follows from the end, the intention of the author. If the author is any good, what he writes about will be determined by his goal. This will determine what is in the book and what is not.

For the commentator on Sacred Scripture, to know the intention of the author will help him understand why something is in it or not. This would be true of historical narratives such as the Gospels, of letters such as St. Paul's, or of the prophecies of the Old Testament. A list of stories or topics might answer the question, "What is in this book?" But that is not quite the same as asking, "What is this book about?" If the answer to that question is a list—the author says this, and then he says that, and then he goes on to say the next thing—it is an inadequate answer. We do want to know the content, but we also want to know what holds all that content together.

Such is St. Thomas's understanding of the matter of a book. It is another way of getting at the *sententiae*, the ideas. Words signify, and ultimately the goal is that they come together to communicate an idea, a *sententia*. What is the central idea of a given book? That idea may itself have many related ideas that themselves contribute to the matter of a book, rather like organs to a body. If we were to ask a reader of a given Gospel what it is about and he responded with a list of stories about Jesus, we would have our inadequate answer. If the answer were simply that it is about Jesus, we would have made progress; a Gospel has Jesus as the subject matter, and then the specific stories would also be the matter in relation to the principal matter of Jesus.

The Division of the Text

St. Thomas regularly makes use of a remarkable tool for articulating the matter: the division of the text. It is commonly used by St. Thomas and his contemporaries in their commentaries on all kinds of books, including Scripture. The division of the text is conceptually quite simple.

When dividing the text, the commentator first states the intention of the author. The commentator thus begins with a conceptual unity to the book as a whole based on what he understands the intention of the author to be. That intention provides the conceptual unity for understanding the book, and thus also for understanding the commentary.

Having stated the author's intention, the commentator then begins to divide the text. The division is like an outline of the entire book. With the intention stated, the commentator provides an initial division of the book into some number of parts related to that intention. He then divides each of the parts into further parts until he has so divided the text that the unit before him is the verse (or less). With this outline in mind, the commentator proceeds through each part or division of his commentary. In the case of St. Thomas, when he comments by way of division (which is most of the time), much of his commentary is given over to laying out the division.

In commenting on the Gospel of St. Matthew, for example, St. Thomas states that St. Matthew treats principally the humanity of Christ. Since it is in his humanity that Christ entered the world, progressed through the world, and then departed from it, St. Thomas divides the Gospel into three parts: the entrance of Christ in his humanity into the world (chs. 1–2), his progress through it (chs. 3–20), and his departure from it (ch. 21 to the end).[1] It is a clear and tidy division, and as St. Thomas proceeds

---

[1] *Super Matt* 1:1, lec. 1, Marietti no. 11.

through his commentary, he divides each section into smaller and smaller parts, all the way down to individual verses.

The division of the text provides a unified vision of the whole of the book (e.g., the humanity of Christ for the Gospel of Matthew). It provides it in the articulation of the very conceptual structure of the book based on the end or goal. In a carefully constructed division of the text, no passage of the book stands alone and disconnected; instead, it stands in a set of nested relations. It is related to the author's intention; it is also related to the passages immediately before it and after it; it is related to passages chapters away. It is, in fact, related to the whole of the book considered in its totality and in all of its parts. A commentator with a good division of the text never answers the matter question with "the author says this, then he says that, then he goes on to say the other thing," as if the book were a string of discrete and disjointed bits. With a good division of the text, the part is always in relation to the whole and the whole is always in relation to its parts.

What might seem at first like trite and tedious carving of the letter is of great importance if one is to understand St. Thomas's commentaries. These divisions give the reader St. Thomas's understanding of the order of thought in the book. Because of that, the division is itself a substantive commentary that is presumed in the explicit commentary on a given passage or verse. It is not uncommon for modern students of the Middle Ages to be disappointed by St. Thomas's commentaries. The disappointment tends to follow a pattern. A particular passage of Scripture is of interest to the student who turns to Thomas and finds that he has remarkably little to say in commenting on that specific verse. And so it is. In comparison with the holy commentators, Thomas can have a modest word count. This is in part because Thomas is famously frugal in his prose. It is also because he has already done quite a bit of expository work in getting to this point in his commentary. Because a given passage is articulated in relation to the whole and its parts, one must see the commentary on that passage in those relations to understand St. Thomas's commentary. Thomas is not one to repeat what he has said; he presumes his reader recalls or will reread.

This applies not only to what has come before but also to what comes after a passage. If one really wants to understand St. Thomas's commentary on a given passage of Scripture, one would need to appreciate its place in a division that situates it within the book and within the commentary as a whole.

The division of the text sheds light on what Thomas means by the "circumstance of the letter." In considering the criteria for a legitimate reading of the literal sense, St. Thomas puts the criteria in the context of the preservation of the circumstance of the letter. This would mean at least the context of the passage in question. One way to think of the division of the text is the establishment of a particularly full circumstance of the letter. In this case, it is not simply a matter of considering a few verses on either side of the letter, or a block of verses, or even a block of chapters; rather, it is a consideration of its place within the whole of the book. Certainly the circumstance of the letter considered from the vantage point of the division of the text is a potentially full and elaborated idea. In the division of the text in relation to the circumstance of the letter, the commentator attempts to get an ever better bead on just what it is that the words signify.

Just as St. Thomas does not think there is necessarily a single exclusive literal interpretation for a given passage of Scripture, neither does he think there is a single exclusive division of the text. The division of the text was widely used by commentators in Thomas's day. Divisions of books by other commentators survive. St. Bonaventure, for example, also comments on the Gospel according to St. John but with a very different division of the text. There is no sign in Thomas that he thinks his division is the true one and Bonaventure's is not. There is, in fact, no recognition of other divisions.[2] The division of the text is an art; it is a way of making sense of a text, and its use is only as good as the skill and intelligence of the commentator. Why could not some other division of the text provide a fruitful entry to a book, one that would be complementary to others? While commentators may agree on the intention of a book's author, they differ widely in how they divide the text in the light of that intention.

The Division of the Gospel According to St. John

Let us consider an example in a bit more detail. The four Gospels each have Jesus as their subject matter. One would

---

[2] Earlier commentaries did not have a full division of the text, but commentators still articulated parts and elements. One can sometimes find such articulation of parts, for example, in the *Glossa ordinaria*. St. Thomas comments that the *Glossa* presents ch. 13 of the letter to the Hebrews as beginning the section of moral instruction. St. Thomas's fully articulated division of the text situates this moral instruction within a much more carefully considered set of moral instructions going back to ch. 12 that are part of a beautifully articulated division according to faith. See *Super Heb* 13:1, lec. 1, Marietti no. 726; for larger frame, see *Super Heb* 11:1, lec. 1, Marietti no. 551.

think, however, that something more precise might be guiding the writing of the evangelists as each writes his own Gospel. We saw above that St. Thomas thought St. Matthew to be particularly concerned with the humanity of Christ.

When he turns his attention to the Gospel of St. John, St. Thomas shifts the intention. St. John intends principally to "show the divinity of the incarnate Word."[3] While each of the Gospels necessarily considers the divinity of Christ, it is St. John who intentionally turns his attention to showing the divinity of the incarnate Word. St. Thomas states the intention precisely in St. John's language from the opening verses of the Gospel. The focus on the mystery of Christ's divinity suggests why St. Thomas's consideration of St. John as author stressed his perfection as a contemplative, for it is just such contemplative perfection that rendered him such a fitting instrument to write the Gospel that has the mystery of Christ's divinity as its principal intention.[4]

In light of this intention, St. Thomas divides the Gospel into two parts: in the first, St. John presents the divinity of Christ (ch. 1), and in the second he manifests that divinity through those things Christ did in the flesh (chs. 2–25). These two parts are in turn further divided. For example, the second part—the manifestation of Christ's divinity through what he did—is divided into two parts: how Christ manifests his divinity in those things he did while living in the world (chs. 2–11) and how Christ manifests his divinity in his death (chs. 12–21). St. Thomas's

---

[3] *Super Ioan* 1:1, lec. 1, Marietti no. 23.

[4] St. Thomas explicitly links his consideration of St. John as author with end and matter in *Super Ioan*, prol., Marietti no. 10.

initial divisions are explicitly tied to the authorial intention. The manifestation of divinity while living in the world is again divided into two parts: manifesting his dominion over nature (ch. 2) and manifesting the effects of grace (chs. 3–11). Each of these, of course, pertains to divine actions and thus the further manifestation of his divinity. This latter is divided into spiritual regeneration (chs. 3–4) and spiritual benefits conferred on those divinely regenerated (chs. 5–11). These spiritual benefits are, in turn, threefold: spiritual life (ch. 5), spiritual food (ch. 6), and spiritual teaching (chs. 7–11).

The articulation of the division is not by way of narrative. St. Thomas identifies chapters 3 and 4 as about spiritual regeneration, not as the stories of Nicodemus and the Samaritan woman at the well. Spiritual benefits describe seven chapters and their movement (life, food, teaching), not the narrative (the healing at the pool of Bethesda, the feeding of the five thousand, the teaching on the bread of life, Jesus's travels back and forth with miracles, and the contentious teachings in Jerusalem). St. Thomas will comment on each of these stories, but the division provides a conceptual context in light of St. John's intention by which one can understand the stories. We are again in the presence of the *sententia*, the ideas that are being expressed in the letter. One might put the question this way: What is St. John getting at by telling this story?

St. Thomas's division consistently shapes the commentary on a given passage. For example, in St. Thomas's division, the second chapter of John manifests Christ's divinity by showing his dominion over nature. This is obvious enough in the miracle of turning water into wine at Cana, which begins the chapter. But what of the cleansing of the temple that follows it? St. Thomas looks to Christ's words concluding the cleansing in which he speaks of his resurrection, which resurrection is an instance of his dominion over nature, perhaps the greatest. The cleansing of the temple provides the occasion for the announcing of the future miracle, and thus it is fittingly understood in relation to Christ's dominion over nature. For St. Thomas, St. John is not just telling stories about Jesus; St. John has a goal, and he does not fundamentally veer from it. As commentator, St. Thomas's task is to work to understand how each part of the Gospel serves the overarching end of the evangelist. Insofar as the division of the text helps the commentator do this and helps his reader understand it, it is a useful tool.

The Letters of St. Paul

The division of the text can be applied to more than a single book of Scripture. St. Thomas applies it to the letters of St. Paul as a whole.

St. Paul's teaching, St. Thomas states, is the teaching of Christ.[5] When he turns to the division of the letters, he says a bit more precisely that the intention of the letters is the grace of Christ.[6] On the basis of this end, St. Thomas articulates a threefold division of the grace of Christ according to the three kinds of recipients of the letters. The grace of Christ can be considered in Christ himself as the head of the mystical body; St. Paul commends this grace in his letter to the Hebrews. The

---

[5] *Super epistolas s. Pauli*, prol., Marietti no. 10.
[6] *Super epistolas s. Pauli*, prol., Marietti no. 11.

grace of Christ can also be considered in the mystical body. St. Paul commends the grace as it is in the principal members of the mystical body in his letters to prelates (the letters to Timothy and Titus), and he commends the grace of Christ as it is in the mystical body itself (the Church) in his letters to the gentile churches. Then, within the letters to the gentile churches, St. Thomas further distinguishes this grace in the mystical body. It can be considered in itself, and St. Paul does this in his letter to the Romans. It can be considered as it is in the sacraments of grace, and St. Paul does this in his two letters to the Corinthians. In the first he considers the sacraments themselves, in the second the ministers of the sacraments. He excludes superfluous sacraments in the letter to the Galatians, meaning sacraments of the Old Law that some seek to unite to the sacraments of the New. Finally, grace can be considered according to the unity it brings about in the Church. St. Paul considers the establishment of that unity in the letter to the Ephesians, its confirmation and growth in the letter to the Philippians, its defense against errors in the letter to the Colossians, its defense against present persecution in the first letter to the Thessalonians, and its defense against future persecution in the second letter to the Thessalonians.[7]

The division of the letters of St. Paul is very clever, but is it not rather farfetched, given the varied circumstances and occasions of Paul's life and work that gave rise to each of the letters? Are not these circumstances also part of what it means that St. Paul is the author? Do they not also shape the subject matter of

---

[7] *Super epistolas s. Pauli*, prol., Marietti no. 11, which also contains the further distinctions between the letters to prelates.

the letters? St. Thomas is not unaware of the particular historical circumstances of the letters and will speak to them in the course of his commentaries; they are not unimportant. They are not, however, ultimately defining of the matter.

To appreciate what St. Thomas is doing, let us recall how he presents St. Paul as the author, as the agent cause. As discussed in chapter 4, St. Thomas's substantive consideration of St. Paul as author in his prologue to the epistles as a whole takes the form of a commentary on the words of Jesus explaining to Ananias in Damascus why he should go to the blinded Paul: "This man is my chosen vessel, to carry my name to nations and kings and the children of Israel" (Acts 9:15). For St. Thomas, what matters most about St. Paul as author is that Paul is an apostle, a vessel created by Christ to bear his name. As a vessel, he has been given wisdom and charity and a perfection of the virtues so that he might carry the name of Christ. For St. Thomas, the letters are intrinsic to St. Paul "the Apostle," for through his letters, his apostolic reach extends beyond those present to those absent and those yet to come.[8] The letters are the work of St. Paul, of the man who through the grace of Christ has been conformed to Christ in soul and even in his flesh to be an apostle. This reality informs all he does, including his letters. This is what matters most deeply about St. Paul as author.

Does that mean, then, that St. Paul consciously intended a series of letters over several years covering the life of grace in Christ in an essentially systematic way? St. Thomas does not

---

[8] *Super epistolas s. Pauli*, prol., Marietti no. 7.

say. More likely, what we see here is something of St. Thomas's sense of God's providential ordering of things as understood in relation to Scripture. St. Paul is indeed a fitting vessel. That he had what it took to write what he did is a matter of being a fitting instrument. That he could see what each circumstance needed in those to whom he wrote was a sign of his greatness as an apostle conformed to Jesus Christ. That the sum total of the letters that survive accomplished something as remarkable as a delineated exposition of the doctrine of grace in the body of Christ—head and members—is at the very least an expression of how St. Thomas understands divine providence to work and the sophistication of the instrumental causality of the authors.

St. Thomas's application of the division of the text to the whole of the corpus of the letters of St. Paul brings out dramatically a unity in matter across the letters, not just in generic themes, but in an ordered precision such that each contributes significantly not only in itself but also in relation to the whole. Whole and part applies not just to a given letter but to all the letters.

The Division of the Whole of Scripture

If St. Thomas is prepared to apply the division of the text to the whole of the Pauline corpus, how much further is he willing to extend it? Could one apply the division of the text to Scripture as a whole? For Thomas, the answer is yes, and he provides just such a division early in his career.[9]

---

[9] St. Thomas is not alone in proposing a division of the whole of Scripture. Here again, he is indicative of the mind of the Middle Ages.

In his *De commendatione et partitione Sacrae Scripturae*, St. Thomas states that Scripture is more useful than anything else, for all who hold to it come to the life of grace to which Scripture disposes, to the life of justice in works to which Scripture directs, and finally to the life of glory which Scripture promises and to which it leads.[10] On the basis of this divine end, St. Thomas divides the whole of Scripture, for Scripture leads to this life in two ways: by giving precepts and by giving aid.[11] Its giving of precepts through the commandments pertains to the Old Testament, and its giving of aid through the gift of grace bestowed by the Law Giver pertains to the New Testament.

And so St. Thomas divides the Old Testament according to the teaching of the commandments. There are two kinds of commandments: those that bind (such as the laws of a king) and those that encourage (such as the commands of a father who teaches his children). The binding laws, the laws of the king, have two aspects: the actual establishing of the law by the king, on the one hand, and the promulgation of the law with its attendant encouragement to obedience through messengers and heralds, on the other. On this basis, St. Thomas distinguishes commands of kings, heralds, and fathers. The commands of the king are found in the Law; the commands of the heralds are found in the Prophets; and the commands of the fathers are found in the Hagiographers (Holy

---

10 *De commendatione*, Marietti no. 1202.
11 For what follows, see *De commendatione*, Marietti nos. 1203–1208.

Writers).[12] This threefold division of the Old Testament is hardly new with St. Thomas; what St. Thomas articulates is a conceptual distinction on the basis of which he presents a traditional division of the Old Testament in a conceptually coherent way. He will then continue his division along these lines so as to place each of the books of the Old Testament within the division.

St. Thomas then turns to the New Testament, which orders to eternal life not only through commandments but also through gifts of grace. In so speaking, St. Thomas maintains the place of commandment in the Old Testament with regard to eternal life. His division is not one that sets the Old Testament aside but rather unites Old and New, with the New now bringing the gift of grace to that ordering to eternal life. He divides the New Testament into three parts: the source of grace (the Gospels), the power of grace (the letters of Paul), and the unfolding of that power (the remaining books). Christ is the source of grace, and his two natures divide the Gospels. St. John especially considers the divine nature, and the other evangelists treat principally the human nature. The very fluidity of such a division is evident in St. Thomas distinguishing Matthew, Mark, and Luke in two different ways.[13] Although St. Thomas does not provide a further division of the letters of St. Paul here, the place of the letters

---

[12] The division of the Old Testament into Law, Prophets, and Hagiographers (Holy Writers) is found in St. Jerome's "Prolog to the Book of Kings," frequently known as the *prologus galeatus*. Prologues of St. Jerome commonly accompanied the books of Sacred Scripture throughout the Middle Ages, and the *prologus galeatus* was particularly well known, as it provided the division of the Old Testament that St. Thomas here uses in his *De commendatione*.

[13] The two distinctions appeal to the two different ways in which the animal symbols had been applied to the evangelists (*De commendatione*, Marietti no. 1208). He also provides two different ways of dividing the major prophets (*De commendatione*, Marietti no. 1206).

corresponds precisely to St. Thomas's description of the letters in the general prologue to his commentary on St. Paul. St. Thomas then divides the remaining books of the New Testament with regard to the unfolding of grace from the time of the apostles to the second coming of Christ.

While St. Thomas does not pursue this division with a commentary on the entirety of Scripture, he clearly thinks there is a fundamental unity to Scripture and an intelligibility of the whole served by each of the parts. Such unity transcends any human intention: this is entirely the work of the divine author, but the work of a divine author who achieves his end through human authors. The intentions of the divine and human authors can, and certainly do, overlap with regard to specific books, and perhaps even specific sets of books. That there is a further intention with regard to the whole of Scripture in its totality and its full integration of whole and parts is the work of the principal author working through the human instruments.

In the light of this vision of the whole, both in principal and in particular, it behooves the reader of St. Thomas's commentaries to have some sense of where Thomas understood those books upon which he comments to fit within the larger frame of his division of Scripture itself.

Isaiah

When St. Thomas comments on Isaiah, he is quite attentive to the historical circumstances of the prophecy. He divides the text with this in mind. He divides the substance of the prophecy into two parts: threats of divine justice (1:2 through chapter

39) and consolation of divine mercy (chs. 40–66). St. Thomas divides each part into smaller and smaller parts, always with an eye to the overarching prophetic character of threat and consolation, careful to note the various historical circumstances and more importantly the precision of the moral circumstances of the people in relation to God and the Law. This is fitting, given the place of the Prophets in St. Thomas's division of the whole of Scripture, as the books of heralds exhorting to the fulfillment of the Law. And yet, this is not the truest matter of the book.

We have seen already, in discussing the end or usefulness of Isaiah, that St. Thomas reads Isaiah with regard to Christ. He began the prologue to his commentary on Isaiah with a verse from Habakkuk: "Write down the vision and explain it on tablets so that he who reads it will finish the race because what is seen is still far off but will appear in the end" (Hab 2:2–3). Recall that "so that he who reads it will finish the race" expressed the end or usefulness of the book, which St. Thomas described as threefold: Christ as the end or goal of the Law, charity as the end or goal of the precepts, and death as the end or goal of life.

The subject matter of the prophecy is found in the command that begins the quotation from Habakkuk: "Write down the vision."[14] The matter is what the prophet saw, and what he saw principally was the appearance of the Son of God. By the appearance of the Son of God, St. Thomas means the Incarnation itself, that Christ is believed by the world, and his

---

[14] For what follows, see *Super Isa*, prol. (Leonine ed., 28:4).

final appearance in glory. The subject matter is this threefold appearance. The words of Habakkuk, "what is seen is still far off but will appear in the end," apply to this understanding of the matter of Isaiah. Christ was indeed still far off when Isaiah prophesied. He was far off not only in time, with centuries before the Incarnation, but also from man, because of his majesty, as God is so far above man, and because he is so hidden in the plan of the Father. All of this changes with the Incarnation when what was high is made low, when what was hidden is made known, and when what was deferred has already begun to be possessed by the saints. This is the subject matter of Isaiah expressed in the prophecies of the immediate historical circumstances of the prophet.

How does one know this? First and foremost, because this is how the Church reads Isaiah. Because of this matter, Isaiah is read in Advent. This is confirmed in turn by St. Thomas's appeal to the holy commentator St. Jerome, who writes that Isaiah's "entire concern is the coming of Christ and the calling of the nations." These are the words from the brief prologue to Isaiah by St. Jerome that was all but ubiquitous in every copy of Isaiah in the Latin West. St. Thomas also thinks there are good reasons for such a reading in the text of Isaiah, in the very letter itself. We shall see that in the next chapter.

St. Thomas hardly denies the concrete historical circumstances of Isaiah, as his division of the text makes clear. It is the actual historical circumstance that is the occasion for the true matter of Isaiah. In the very threats of divine displeasure and the promises of divine mercy, one finds the essential concern of Isaiah himself, "the coming of Christ and the calling of the nations." For St. Thomas, this matter is Isaiah's. It is not that Isaiah is speaking about one thing and God is really speaking about something else. In the case of the prophets, the prophets have knowledge of what their prophecies are about. To appreciate this requires an understanding of prophetic vision and its implications for the genre of prophecy, which we will consider in the next chapter.

Juxtapositions of the Letter

One of the immediately arresting features of St. Thomas's commentaries is his constant juxtaposition of passages of Scripture. He brings passages from various parts of Scripture to bear on a passage from some other part of Scripture. In doing this, he seems to show a stunning disregard for the circumstance of the letter. While the charge of such disregard may be overstated, we can grant it nonetheless. Such disregard for the circumstance of the letter points us to another way St. Thomas understands Scripture. The point is not simply that, because God is the divine author of Scripture, one can use one part of Scripture to make sense of some other part, although that is certainly true. Something else is at work here. The commentator must do this because of the very enormity and mysteriousness of the end and matter of Scripture. No one passage or book is sufficient to the task. Other parts can be brought to bear such that one illuminates the other to a fuller understanding of the reality revealed.

How should we read the piled up scriptural quotations that populate St. Thomas's commentaries? St. Thomas may do this to affirm that the point made here is made elsewhere. In accord with long standing principles, St. Thomas will use a more explicit passage to confirm an exposition of an opaque passage. More frequently, I think, St. Thomas is up to something different. He recognizes that, whatever this passage of Scripture may be saying, it is not expressing the idea, the *sententia*, in its fullness. The profounder the mystery in question, the truer this is. Such juxtapositions remind his reader not simply that this topic is found elsewhere but that aspects of it are found elsewhere and that a fullness of understanding requires not simply the letter under examination but its consideration in conjunction with others, such as (but presumably not limited to) the ones additionally quoted.

Let us look at some examples. Consider St. Thomas's commentary on these words of St. Paul: "How beautiful are the feet of those heralding peace, of those heralding good things" (Rom 10:15). What is meant by "peace" in this passage? St. Thomas brings out three aspects of peace, each of which is taught by Scripture:

First, they announce the peace which Christ established between men and God, 2 Cor 5:19: "God was in Christ reconciling the world to himself. And he placed the word of reconciliation among us." Rom 5:1: "May we have peace with the Lord through Jesus Christ." Second, they announce the peace that is to be had among all men. Rom 12:18: "If it could happen that there is among you those having peace with all men." Third, they announce those things by which man can have peace in himself. Ps 118:165: "Abundant is peace for those who love your law, O Lord." And under these three is contained all those things in this life that are useful for salvation, either with regard to God, or with regard to neighbor, or with regard to oneself.[15]

As is frequently the case, the immediate link to the other passages is verbal. St. Thomas quotes other passages that speak of peace. This is, of course, not always the case, as with the first quotation from 2 Corinthians, but it is immediately followed by a passage from earlier in Romans that does speak of peace. The question for St. Thomas as commentator is how to understand the peace that is being announced. Thomas's principal recourse is to Scripture itself, and each of the passages he cites brings out a different aspect of peace. No one passage exhausts the reality of peace. St. Thomas's selection covers the breadth of reality to show the fullness of the reach of that peace that is achieved by Christ: peace with God, with neighbor, and with self. In this threefold peace, St. Thomas here sees "all those things in this life that are useful for salvation." This is quite a claim for peace, for one word. St. Thomas's task as commentator is to explain what that word signifies within the circumstance of the letter. He sees the richness and depth of what St. Paul is communicating.

St. Thomas could have said all of this without any appeal to Scripture. That these are attributes of peace found in

---

[15] *Super Rom* 10:15, lec. 2, Marietti no. 841.

Scripture certainly gives the ideas greater authority, but I seriously doubt that St. Thomas is scrambling for Scriptural authority for his own ideas about peace. Rather, the very understanding of peace that he brings to bear on this passage of Romans is itself already formed by his reading of Scripture. That these are true and fitting aspects of the reality of peace, especially the peace achieved by Christ, is made known by Scripture in the first place. Notably, St. Thomas appeals to the end of Scripture that "under these three is contained all those things in this life that are useful for salvation." Scripture illuminates, unites, and orders these three aspects of peace to the end of man's salvation.

We find another threefold peace in St. Thomas's commentary on Christ's greeting of "peace be with you" to his disciples after the Resurrection:

> He greets them with the words of salutation, saying
> "Peace be with you." This was necessary because their
> peace had been perturbed in several ways. First with
> regard to God, against whom some had sinned by
> denying him, and some by fleeing, Matt 26:31: "You
> have all suffered scandal in me this night, for it is
> written, strike the shepherd and disperse the sheep
> of the flock." Against this he offers them the peace of
> reconciliation with God—Rom 5:10: "We have been
> reconciled with God through the death of His son"—
> for he accomplished this through the Passion. Second
> with regard to themselves, because they were sad and
> doubtful in faith, and this peace too he offered them,

Ps. 118:165: "Peace is great for those who love your law." Finally with regard to outsiders, because they were suffering persecution from the Jews, and against this he said to them, "Peace be with you," namely, against the persecutions of the Jews, John 14:27: "My peace I give you, my peace I leave you."[16]

The three senses of peace are similar to those St. Thomas spells out in commenting on St. Paul but more precise, given the circumstance of Christ's appearance to all but Thomas after his Passion and death. Here too he begins with the peace that is reconciliation with God, a reconciliation he has just accomplished in his Passion and death, so fittingly indicated by the quotation from Romans. The second peace is with regard to their sadness and doubt by which they lacked peace in themselves—again, a peace that is especially to be offered by the risen Christ. Finally, he offers a peace with regard to others, here precisely the Jews whose persecution they feared.

Jesus's greeting of "peace be with you" a second time when the apostle Thomas is present gets a different set of three juxtapositions:

John shows Christ's mode of speaking in "Peace be with you," namely, the peace of reconciliation with God that he proclaimed accomplished, Rom 5:10: "We have been reconciled with God through the death of his son." Col 1:20: "Pacifying through the blood of his Cross what is

---

[16] *Super Ioan* 20:19, lec. 4, Marietti no. 2532.

in heaven or what is on earth." Second, the future peace of eternity and immortality that he promised them they will have, Ps 147:14: "Who established peace on your borders." And third, the peace of charity and unity which he commanded them to preserve, Mark 9:49: "Have peace among yourselves."[17]

St. Thomas here again begins with the peace that is the reconciliation of man with God. So he begins each of his commentaries on peace, and we may have a glimpse into St. Thomas's understanding of peace as first and foremost necessarily founded in the reconciliation of man with God accomplished by Christ. The second peace looks to eternity and the third to charity and unity, each among the effects of what Christ's death and resurrection have accomplished. If the first greeting of peace to his apostles was particularly addressed to the circumstances of anxiety and fear that followed upon Christ's death, this second set is more focused on the peace that follows from the resurrection and is to mark their lives as his apostles after the ascension.

In these commentaries, we see that such juxtaposition of passages is an art. Scripture has much to say about peace. Thomas selects the particular passages in such a way as to illuminate peace within the context of the passage in question. Also notable in these passages, and consistent throughout St. Thomas's commentaries, is that he does little if anything to explain the juxtapositions. He leaves it for the reader to see,

---

[17] *Super Ioan* 20:26, lec. 6, Marietti no. 2554.

indeed to meditate, on the juxtapositions. This is a potentially fruitful exercise for those who have much of Scripture already committed to memory.

Let us turn to a particularly dramatic and illuminating instance of this practice. Chapters 24–50 of St. Thomas's commentary on Isaiah survive in his own handwriting. St. Thomas writes his commentary in two columns on each page. He also writes notes in the margins of this manuscript, notes that have come to be called "collations." These collations are juxtapositions of Scripture passages in the form of diagrams. A particularly notable one is found at the end of his commentary on chapter 40. In Thomas's division of Isaiah, chapter 40 begins the consolation of Judah, which extends to the end of the book. This consolation takes the form of the promise of many good things. In the course of this glorious opening proclamation of both the power of the one who will comfort and the comfort of what he promises, we read: "But they that hope in the Lord shall renew their strength, they shall take wings as eagles, they shall run and not be weary, they shall walk and not faint" (Isa 40:31). The phrase "they shall take wings as eagles" is treated briefly in the commentary itself according to St. Thomas's practice. But Thomas has more on his mind when it comes to those who shall take wings as eagles. It is these eagles that prompt a diagram at the bottom of the page.[18]

Need we say that the verse is not really about eagles but a metaphor? Those who hope in the Lord are compared to eagles. Who are those who hope in the Lord? The saints. What

---

[18] *Super Isa* 40:31 (Leonine ed., 28:172); see accompanying diagram.

St. Thomas's Diagram of Eagles in His Commentary on Isaiah 40:31

saiah 40:31: "But they that hope in the Lord shall renew their strength, they shall take wings
as eagles, they shall run and not be weary, they shall walk and not faint."

The saints are compared to eagles:

—on account of the height of their flight, Job 39, "will at your command, etc."
[39:27, 29: "Will at your command the eagle mount up and make her nest in the high places? . . .
From thence she looks for food, her eyes behold afar off."]
in which is the eminence of contemplation, Isa 33, "the king in his beauty, etc."
[33:17: "His eyes shall see the king in his beauty, they shall see the land far off."]

—on account of the subtlety of fragrance, Luke 16, "wheresoever the body shall be, etc."
[17:37: "Wheresoever the body shall be, there will the eagles also be gathered together."]
in which is the fervor of love, Song 1, "draw me after you, etc."
[1:3: "Draw me: we will run after you to the fragrance of your ointments."]

—on account of the sublimity of place, Prov 30, "three things are hard to me, etc."
[30:18: "Three things are hard to me and the fourth I am utterly ignorant of. The way of an eagle
in the air, the way of a serpent upon a rock, the way of a ship in the midst of the sea, and the way
of a man in his youth."]
in which is the zeal for the heavenly way of life [conversation], Phil 3, "our conversation, etc."
[3:20: "Our conversation is in heaven, from whence also we look for the savior, our Lord Jesus
Christ."]

—on account of the swiftness of motion, Lam 4, "were swifter, etc."
[4:19: "Our persecutors were swifter than the eagles of the air."]
in which is the promptness of good action, Prov 22, "have you seen a man, etc."
[22:29: "Have you seen a man swift in his work? He shall stand before kings and shall not be before
those that are lowborn."]

—on account of renewal, Ps, "shall be renewed like the eagle's, etc."
[102:5: "Your youth shall be renewed like the eagle's."]
[Note: Thomas often will cite "Psalm" without the psalm number.]
in which is zeal for correction and progress, 2 Cor 4, "although the outward man, etc."
[4:16: "Although the outward man is corrupted, yet the inward man is renewed day by day."]

—on account of the beauty of the parts, Ezek 17, "a large eagle, etc."
[17:3: "A large eagle with great wings, long-limbed, full of feathers and of variety, came to Libanus
and took away of the marrow of the cedar."]
in which is the beauty of virtues, Song 4, "you are all beautiful, etc."
[4:7: "You are all beautiful, O my friend, and there is not a spot in you. Come from Libanus, my
spouse, come from Libanus."]

—on account of the solicitude of children, Deut 32, "as the eagle enticing, etc."
[32:11: "As the eagle enticing her young to fly and hovering over them, he spreads his wings and
has taken him and carried him on his shoulders."]
in which is the solicitude of the saints, 2 Cor 11, "who is weak, etc."
[11:29: "Besides those things which are without, my daily urgency is the solicitude of all the
churches. Who is weak and I am not weak? Who is scandalized, and I am not on fire?"]

follows illuminates how St. Thomas's mind works. We have seven scriptural passages—or more properly, we have seven short phrases intended to trigger St. Thomas's memory—each of which speaks to a natural attribute of eagles: they make their nests at great heights from whence they can see great distances; they have an acute sense of smell (or so Thomas seems to mean); they fly to high places; they fly swiftly; they renew themselves; they are beautiful in their proportion; and they are solicitous of their young, carrying them on their shoulders. The power of the medieval memory is such that the short quotations do not necessarily mention eagles; the few words are enough to jog St. Thomas's memory to recall the whole passage and get to the actual mention of eagles. Thus each of these natural attributes of the eagle is attested to by Scripture. It is not, I would think, that St. Thomas has no confidence in the ability of human observation to determine the attributes of eagles; rather, it is that, if one is to apply the attributes metaphorically to the saints, it is good to ground them in the attributes of eagles as also found in Scripture. Thus he not only states attributes but attributes found in Scripture.

On the basis of each natural attribute found in Scripture, Thomas attributes some spiritual attribute to the saints: from the heights of the eagle's nest, the eminence of what the contemplative beholds; from their acute senses, the fervor of the love that draws him; from the heights of their flight, his zeal for holiness; from the swiftness of their flight, the promptness of his good actions; from their renewal, his zeal to correct his faults and advance in the spiritual life; from their beauty in proportion, the beauty of his virtues; and finally, from their solicitude for their young, his solicitude and care for others. Each of these, in turn, is confirmed as an attribute of the saint by another short passage from Scripture intended to jog St. Thomas's memory. The movement is thus twofold: the gathered natural attributes of the eagle, which are then applied metaphorically to the spiritual attributes of the saint.

St. Thomas's diagram is illuminative of his reading of Scripture. He takes the things signified by the word seriously. He takes eagles seriously. One can imagine easily enough that St. Thomas has knowledge of eagles from his reading of natural history and from his own experience. He is also reading Scripture very carefully with regard to the actual words. Although the Dominicans were preparing a concordance in the thirteenth century, St. Thomas does not seem to need one. He has most, probably all, of Scripture committed to memory. He can just jot a bit of a phrase down and that is enough. Such is common in citations throughout St. Thomas's commentaries and the commentaries of others. Citations are always verbal, a word or two to jog the memory. Chapter numbers, when provided, are bonus and not necessarily correct. The textual memory is more reliable. And so St. Thomas considers manifold instances of the eagle in Scripture, and he does so precisely with regard to the thing signified by the word: "eagle." Such study and meditation would be, I would think, itself a delight for St. Thomas in thinking about the things of God's creation.

What prompts the particular diagram in Isaiah, however, is a metaphor. The saint is being compared to the eagle. How to understand that metaphor? One needs to start with the thing itself that is the basis of the comparison. The point of a metaphor is to make something better understood, for the better one understands the thing itself, the better one can apply it to the thing being described by the metaphor. The better one understands eagles, the better one can understand the saint.[19] One finds throughout St. Thomas's commentaries this great delight in words and things.

◆

As we consider St. Thomas's understanding of the material cause of Scripture, the matter, we see yet again a richness and complexity. The matter ranges across all of creation and providence. It is inextricably bound with the end and usefulness of Scripture and with the authors both divine and human. Precisely because of the divine author, creation is present in its delightful particulars. Those particulars come to be seen in increasingly manifold ways of fullness as, in the light of Scripture, they are seen ever more clearly in relation to the end of Scripture, which is the end and goal of all things in relation to God.

---

[19] That this diagram is the most developed among the collations in St. Thomas's commentary on Isaiah may, perhaps, be related to the identification of the eagle with St. John, that master of contemplation. One might also note that the description of the saint in this collation fits exquisitely the mix of the contemplative life and the active life that is the mark of the Dominican way of life.

CHAPTER 6

HOW? LITERARY STYLE (*FORMA SEU MODUS*)

Form

When St. Thomas considers animals, he considers two intrinsic causes: matter and form. The matter is the body and its parts; the form is the soul. The soul is the animating principal of the animal, as indeed our English "animation" comes from the Latin word for "soul," *anima*. What does animating mean? The soul makes it living, which is to say that it unites all of the parts of the body into a unified whole that is a single living acting thing. Without the soul, there is no unified thing, just a sack of organs, and in fact a sack of organs that is decomposing (like a corpse), coming apart, because there is no soul.

How does St. Thomas understand form in the case of a literary work such as a book? In the light of end, author, and matter, we could ask this question: What does it take for this author to communicate this subject matter to achieve his goal, to make this material useful? Is there an intrinsic principle that holds the matter together, that gives order to its parts, that gives it shape? The answer is what St. Thomas calls *modus* and we might call "genre" and "style" and "literary technique." How does an author communicate? In narrative, in dialog, in poetry, or by way of metaphor or irony or argument. One could communicate the same subject matter in a variety of different ways. Still, subject matter and genre are so intimately related that together they constitute one thing. That is why we can answer the "what?" question in terms of genre. What is it? It is a dialog; it is an epic poem. But when we give that answer, we usually need to specify it further with regard to subject matter (a dialog about the nature of justice or an epic poem about the founding of Rome), suggesting both the fitting distinction between matter and genre and their necessary conjunction in reality.

Style

The commentator on Scripture must be attentive to style. Prophecy differs from history.[1] Wisdom literature differs from apocalyptic literature. One ought not read a parable as one reads history. St. Thomas knows this, as do the holy commentators. Medieval commentators might disagree as to the style of a particular book or passage. None would argue that genre or style do not matter.

---

[1] *Super Isa* 1:1 (Leonine ed., 28:8).

In the prologue to his commentary on the Psalms, St. Thomas says that multiple styles are found in Scripture, and he names four. The first is narrative, and it is found in historical books. In the second place is a cluster: preceptive, admonitory, and exhortatory. Preceptive is found in the Law, admonitory in the Prophets, and exhortatory in the books of Solomon. We can recognize these from St. Thomas's division of the Old Testament with regard to king, herald, and father in relation to commandment. Thus St. Thomas's division of the Old Testament according to subject matter can also be articulated as a division according to style. The third style is disputative and is found in Job and the Apostle Paul. The fourth style is deprecatory or laudatory, which is to say, petition or praise. This is the style of the Psalms. Such in broad terms is a distinction of the styles of Scripture. Again, we ought not to be too fussy. St. Paul says in the opening verse of the letter to the Hebrews that God had spoken to our fathers in many ways. In commenting on these "many ways," St. Thomas says that there is no way of speaking (*modi loquendi*) that is not found in the Old Testament.[2] Even the four that St. Thomas presents in his prologue to the Psalms are in fact seven. There are many styles. Let us consider more closely how St. Thomas understands the place of style in Scripture.

Disputative Style in Job

St. Thomas says that the style of Job is that of disputation. End, matter, and form all come together in St. Thomas's reading of

---

[2] *Super Heb* 1:1, lec. 1, Marietti no. 9.

Job. The book of Job is, according to St. Thomas, about divine providence, specifically divine providence over men. The whole intention of the book is to show by probable arguments that human affairs are ruled by divine providence.[3] St. Thomas is clear as to the usefulness of this intention: reverence, fear, and love of God are all lost when divine providence over human affairs is denied. When man loses reverence, fear, and love of God, he all too easily falls away from virtue and inclines to vice. The most pointed challenge to divine providence in human affairs is the suffering of the just, and Job is precisely about that. Thus the intention and the usefulness are clear.

How does the author go about fulfilling this intention? By way of disputation: this is a book of probable arguments. Job is also a story. For the sake of the argument, it does not really matter whether the story is true or not. Authors will sometimes make up stories in order to present arguments. Even if the argument does not depend on whether Job was real or not, St. Thomas insists that he was real because he is presented as real elsewhere in Scripture. The critical point for St. Thomas with regard to mode is that the story is in the service of the argument. Thus, while St. Thomas carefully follows the story in his commentary, it is first and foremost in the service of the disputation.[4]

The commentary on Job is the only commentary in which St. Thomas does not employ a division of the text. It is apparently not useful to St. Thomas's purpose as a commentator. The commentary proceeds very carefully according to

---

[3] *Super Iob*, prol. (Leonine ed., 26:3). See the prologue for what follows.
[4] See *Super Iob* 1:1 (Leonine ed., 26:5).

the argument, but an argument that arises from a story. St. Thomas does not just harvest the argument and then discard the story. It is a mark of St. Thomas's skill as a commentator that both argument and story are in play but in an ordered way. St. Thomas never loses sight of the argument or its purpose: probable arguments for the governance of human affairs by divine providence. He reads Job as a kind of disputed question between Job and his friends. The disputed question—that exquisite formal exercise of the medieval schools—provides a fruitful contemporary image for Thomas and his readers. St. Thomas, always the master of argument, is a sure guide to the argument and its movement throughout his commentary.

At the same time, the argument is in the context of a story, and St. Thomas never simply sets the story aside. Because he is such a good reader of the arguments, he sees that the argument of Job's comforters sometimes stalls; they do not actually move the argument forward. They fail to understand Job's arguments and simply repeat their own arguments that Job has already addressed. How can that be? This is why St. Thomas does not simply harvest the argument and cast off the story. The story of Job and his dispute with his friends is a moral story. How is it that one does not hear the arguments of another with understanding? For St. Thomas, Job is not a book of gussied up arguments; it is a true dialog in which the moral character of the participants matters. That too is part of the story and plays a role in the disputation and the movement of the argument. St. Thomas's attention to the mode of disputation assists him in bringing out a secondary aspect of the subject matter. Yes, first and foremost, this is about getting providence right. But in so doing, one also learns about getting disputation right. It is about the holiness of Job—always *Beatus Job* for St. Thomas, as for the tradition, because it is the very title of the book in Latin—and the ways in which moral and spiritual weakness can affect intellectual understanding.

Paul's Letters as Disputation

When speaking of books that are argumentative in their form, St. Thomas points to both Job and the letters of St. Paul. A disputative style or mode is perhaps relatively obvious for Job, and the argument unfolds in a relatively clear and orderly way between the disputants of the story. That St. Thomas also includes the letters of St. Paul tells us something about the way St. Thomas reads those letters. As a matter of genre, are they not letters? Yes, and St. Thomas is aware of it.[5] He says at one point in commenting on the letter to the Hebrews that letters ought to tell stories briefly.[6] He readily distinguishes the salutation from the body of the letter in his divisions of the text. But there are many kinds of letters doing many kinds of things, and saying that the letters of St. Paul are argumentative in style is to specify the kind of letters.

This is particularly important for readers of St. Thomas's commentaries on the letters of St. Paul. St. Thomas understands St. Paul as making arguments. That St. Paul is doing this is not always obvious. For many a reader of St. Paul, his mind seems to be firing in many directions all at once; the ideas are

---

[5] In his general prologue to his commentary on the letters of St. Paul, St. Thomas says the genre is letters; see *Super epistolas s. Pauli*, prol., Marietti no. 10.
[6] *Super Heb* 11:32, lec. 7, Marietti no. 628.

tumbling out on the page. While they are related, is there really an argument? For St. Thomas, the answer is yes. The reader who loses sight of the letters as argumentative in form readily gets lost in St. Thomas's commentaries. We can appreciate what St. Thomas is doing in his commentaries if we revisit his use of "intention."

Intention of the Author Revisited[7]

St. Thomas frequently speaks of St. Paul's intention. We need to be careful not to take this in a general sense as "St. Paul's meaning." St. Thomas uses it in a precise way in presenting Paul's arguments. St. Thomas may be convinced that St. Paul makes arguments in his letters, but he concedes that the arguments are not always made with the completeness and in a form designed to satisfy professors of philosophy. Premises are missing, and sometimes conclusions are missing. Paul can digress from the main argument and not inform his reader either of the digression or of the return to the main argument. Sometimes the arguments are simply difficult.[8] St. Thomas has a love and a nose for argument. He works hard in his commentaries on the letters of Paul to bring out the specific arguments of the Apostle. In so doing, he does what any good philosopher will do in such a circumstance: he states the conclusion to be had. One can get a handle on an argument much more readily if one knows the conclusion. Knowing the conclusion is essential if one is trying to make implicit premises explicit,

---

[7] Picking up from the "Intention of the Author" section in chapter 3.

[8] In *Super Heb* 13:10, lec. 2, Marietti no. 743, St. Thomas notes an argument in the letter to the Hebrews that is "especially subtle."

or if one is simply trying to figure out how the various statements tumbling from St. Paul's pen are, in fact, related. It is a mark of Thomas's genius as a commentator on St. Paul that he is always on the look out for the argument and patiently sifting the Apostle's prose for it. He then guides his reader to understand the line of argument. To do this, Thomas is clear to state the conclusion to which Paul is working. Thomas speaks of this conclusion as the "intention." It is the end or goal of the argument, whether for an argument over the course of chapters or just a few verses. If the conclusion is clear, one can see how the rest is ordered to it, which is precisely the function of intention. Intention is about the end, and in the case of arguments, the end is the conclusion. That is where the argument is going. When St. Thomas speaks about what St. Paul intends, he does not speak to the meaning of St. Paul's words but rather to the conclusion by means of which the commentator can come to see more clearly and precisely the meaning of the words.

St. Paul, Argument, and Theology

In his general prologue to the letters of St. Paul, St. Thomas says that they contain nearly the whole teaching of theology.[9] To understand what St. Thomas could possibly mean, let us consider briefly what he takes theology to be.[10] St. Thomas teaches that theology is a science. By science, St. Thomas means an ordered body of knowledge. A science is ordered when it considers its subject matter according to the causes that are proper to the things being studied. So how

---

[9] *Super epistolas s. Pauli*, prol., Marietti no. 7.
[10] For what follows, see *ST* I, q. 1.

is theology a science? It strives to give order to what God has revealed. The faithful want to understand what God has revealed. That understanding deepens when one understands how the revealed truths are related one to another, and those relations are at their most illuminating and profound when they are causal. For St. Thomas, theology proceeds by way of argument, meaning that, on the basis of understanding one revealed truth in its causal power, the theologian should be able to conclude to another revealed truth. The theologian argues from one revealed truth to another and, in so doing, shows the relation of one truth to another. First and foremost, the theologian does not argue for new theological truths from revelation; he argues from revelation to revelation to better understand the deep causal realities that unite what God has revealed. He strives to see and understand the unity in what God has revealed in Jesus Christ. All of this presumes that the theologian is a believer. In confessing the true faith—"My Lord and my God" (John 20:28)—the apostle Thomas was made immediately a good theologian.[11]

St. Thomas asks in his *Summa theologiae* whether sacred teaching, theology, proceeds by way of argument.[12] The answer is yes, and his example is St. Paul when he argues for the universal resurrection of the dead from the resurrection of Jesus Christ. This is a true argument because, if one understands the causal power of Christ's resurrection, at least in part, one sees in it the cause of the universal resurrection of the dead. St. Paul knows this and argues from the former to the latter. St. Paul

---

[11] *Super Ioan* 20:28, lec. 6, Marietti no. 2562.
[12] *ST* I, q. 1, a. 8.

is not creating new theological truths; he is showing how two revealed truths, the resurrection of Christ and the universal resurrection of the dead, are intrinsically and causally related. This is the work of the theologian. For St. Thomas, St. Paul is an exemplary theologian.

When St. Thomas says that the mode of St. Paul's letters is argument, he has this capacious understanding of the work of the theologian in mind. When he says that the letters have the teaching of Christ for their matter or that they contain nearly the whole of theology, he does not mean that there is a remarkably big pile of stuff in the letters. He means that the letters contain much—nearly the whole of theology—but it is not a pile. It is ordered, and it is ordered according to the demands of the human mind—indeed, ordered to the require-ments of wisdom—for these truths are understood in relation to their causes, and ultimately the highest cause, which is God. St. Paul brings out any number of causal relationships between the revealed truths of faith so that the faithful may understand those truths all the more deeply. St. Thomas' task as commenta-tor is to articulate those causal relationships brought out by St. Paul, and that means following the lines of argument.

The Psalms

Let us consider a different book and a different style. As noted above, St. Thomas describes the style of the Psalms as petition or praise. He begins his prologue to his commentary with a verse from Ecclesiasticus/Sirach, "In every work, he confessed to the holy and exalted one in the word of glory"

(Sir 47:9).[13] These words are said literally of David himself and manifest the fourfold cause of the book of Psalms. In commenting on it, St. Thomas makes some notable claims for the Psalter.

"In every work" expresses the universal subject matter of the Psalms. St. Thomas quotes Dionysius's *De coelesti hierarchia* (On the Celestial Hierarchy): "Sacred Scripture intends in the divine fragrances of the Psalms to sing of the whole of divine and sacred works."[14] Thomas articulates a fourfold divine work by way of verbal links to God's "work" as described in Scripture. First, "for God rested on the seventh day from all his work" (Gen 2:2) speaks of the work of creation. Second, "my Father is working yet until now" (John 5:17) speaks of God's governance of what he created. Third, "my food is to do the will of him who sent me that I might complete his work" (John 4:34) speaks of the work of reparation. And finally, "the work of the Lord is filled with his glory" (Sir 42:16) speaks of the work of glorification. Such are the works of God from the beginning to the end: creation, providence, reparation, and final glorification. St. Thomas does not say that these are all touched on in the Psalms; one would think all are more or less touched on in various ways in each book of Scripture. St. Thomas says, rather, that all of these are treated completely in the teaching of the Psalms. Thus the proper subject, the matter, of the Psalms is universal because it treats of all the works of God completely.

In the light of this completeness, St. Thomas says that the

---

[13] For what follows, see *In Psalmos*, prooemium (Parma ed., 14:148).

[14] Actually from Dionysius, *De ecclesiastica hierarchia* (*On the Ecclesiastical Hierarchy*), chapter 3.

Psalter contains the whole of Sacred Scripture and has as its matter the "whole of theology." Because the Psalter contains the whole of Scripture, it is found so frequently in the Church. In the liturgical life of the Church in the Middle Ages, the Psalms were omnipresent; they were the backbone of the divine office sung by religious throughout the Church, including, of course, St. Thomas. They still are. St. Thomas says that one reason they are recited so frequently is that the whole of Scripture is found in them. One may not be able to read all of Scripture (many a poor library no doubt lacked parts of Scripture, as the whole of Scripture consisted of many manuscripts and was very expensive), but one could have all that Scripture teaches if one had the Psalter. It is a remarkable claim.

St. Thomas goes still further. "And because all this work pertains to Christ—'in him it was pleasing that the fullness of divinity should dwell' (Col 1:19)—the matter of this book is thus Christ and his members." If the Psalms are about every work of God and the fullness of God is in Jesus Christ the head and the Church his members, then the Psalms most profoundly have Christ, head and members, as their subject.

St. Thomas makes the same claim for totality of teaching in the Psalms as he made for St. Paul's letters.[15] If the matter is the same—the works of God most profoundly in Christ—then how do we distinguish the two? One answer is style. St. Paul's letters proceed by way of argument. In the quotation from Ecclesiasticus with which St. Thomas begins his prologue to his commentary on the Psalms, David "confesses." How

---

[15] He speaks of the two together in this way in his general prologue to his commentary on the letters of St. Paul; see *Super epistolas s. Pauli*, prol., Marietti no. 6.

does he do that? With psalms, which St. Thomas describes as the praise of God with song that elevates the mind to eternal things. St. Thomas says the style of the Psalms is petition and praise; he also says the style is praise and prayer. St. Paul argues; David prays.

There are two senses of prayer at work in St. Thomas's consideration of the Psalms. The first is prayer as a literary style. The second is prayer as the end or goal of those hymns that are prayers. The goal of prayer is the elevation of the mind to God. In the words of Ecclesiasticus, David "confessed to the holy and exalted one." In his confessing, he is raised to the holy and exalted one. St. Thomas describes four ways the soul is raised to God: the soul is raised to the admiration of the heights of divine power by faith; the soul is raised to striving for the excellence of eternal beatitude by hope; the soul is raised to dwelling in the divine goodness and holiness by charity; and the soul is raised to the imitation of divine justice in deeds by justice. Thus the Psalms raise up the soul in faith, hope, charity, and justice by hymns of praise and petition that have as their matter the totality of the divine works of God in Jesus Christ. Such governs St. Thomas's reading of the Psalms. The style is at the heart of his reading of the Psalms, for when the psalms are truly prayers, they are indeed the raising of the soul to God.[16] In this, St. Thomas expresses what is the lived reality of the Church: she prays the Psalms.

This understanding of the Psalter shapes St. Thomas's

---

[16] Again, St. Thomas is not a slave to his own categories. He is only to the second psalm when he notes that it does not fit the style: "It should be noted that this whole psalm contains nothing of prayer" (*In Psalmos* 2 [Parma ed., 14:152, no. 1]).

division of the text. He notes different ways the Psalms have been divided and then begins the division that will govern his commentary. He divides the Psalms into three groups of fifty each. This distinction reflects the threefold state of the people of faith: repentance, justice, and the praise of eternal glory. Each section is signaled by its concluding psalm. St. Thomas comments on only the first fifty-four psalms, and that is enough for us to see that he is far from rigid in forcing every verse of every psalm into the spiritual state corresponding to the section. Rather, the states of repentance, justice, and praise of eternal glory suggest something thematic. After all, the Psalms contain the whole of theology and Scripture. In St. Thomas's rich reading of the Psalms, the division according to states of life helps give shape and insight into the many mysteries expressed in the book. Let us recall St. Thomas's understanding of the end or goal of the Psalms as prayer, as the raising of the heart to God. In that light, it is fitting that he would find in the structure of the Psalter the threefold ordered spiritual states of man.

Still, these psalms of prayer are by David; they have historical circumstances. Has St. Thomas abandoned the author and his history? What is the relationship between the universal matter of all of Scripture and the actual historical circumstances of which David concretely speaks in at least some of his psalms? That history is at work in St. Thomas's division of the text. The first fifty psalms, as noted, pertain to the spiritual state of repentance. St. Thomas finds this theme in the historical tribulations and battles of David that occasion at least some of these psalms.[17] As king, David prays against two kinds of attack and persecution. There is attack against the whole people, and this is in the last decade (Psalms 41–50). Then there is attack against the just man. This is twofold: direct attack in temporal matters and indirect attack by those who live their lives unjustly. This second kind is the subject of the fourth decade (Psalms 31–40). David the king suffered direct attack against himself both from specific persons and from the whole people. David's prayers against attacks from the whole people are the subject of the third decade (Psalms 21–30). With regard to attack at the hands of specific persons, David suffered at the hands of both Saul and Absalom. The persecution of Saul is the subject of the second decade (Psalms 11–20) and the persecution of Absalom the subject of the first decade. St. Thomas's very division of the text is attentive to the historical circumstances of David.

That the Psalms are about more than David's historical circumstances, however, is indicated in the historical material itself. One indication is the order of that material, for although the Psalms speak of historical events, they do not treat them in historical order. David writes Psalm 3 when he flees from Absalom; he writes Psalm 17 when he is freed from the hands of Saul. The latter happened before the former. St. Thomas concludes: "These psalms signify something more than history alone." History has an order, and if it is not being followed, there must be a reason. The inversion of the historical order is an indication to the attentive reader that he is in

---

[17] For the division that follows, see *In Psalmos*, prooemium (Parma ed., 14:150).

the presence of divine mystery. The inversion of the historical order is so significant for St. Thomas that he divided the text according to it.

When St. Thomas introduces David and his history to establish the literal division of the text, he also says that David is treated figuratively. With David, we have one of the most consistently developed figures in the work of St. Thomas and indeed in the entire tradition. St. Jerome handed down a rule that St. Thomas says he will follow in his commentary on the Psalms, that the historical deeds of the Psalms are to be explained as figures of something about Christ and his Church. St. Thomas actually has a Latin verb: the historical deeds are to be explained as "figuring" something about Christ and his Church.[18] It may be a rule of St. Jerome, but St. Thomas does not need a rule; his mind thinks habitually in terms of figures, especially of figures that point ultimately to Christ and his Church.

What does St. Thomas mean when he says David is a figure of Christ? David signifies Christ because there is something about David (perhaps many things) that are like Christ as a pattern or model or characteristic. David is a king, and the very circumstances of that kingdom have already been used to divide the first fifty psalms. In the course of his commentary, St. Thomas will develop the historical reality as a figure of Christ and his Church. The circumstances of David and his psalms can thus signify Christ and in signifying Christ can also signify his body the Church. St. Thomas does not look simply

---

[18] *In Psalmos,* prooemium (Parma ed., 14:149).

to historical events. In considering the kingdom of David as a figure of the Kingdom of Christ, for example, St. Thomas says that Christ is fittingly signified by David and this in two ways: David is mighty and handsome. Christ is the power of God and the splendor of the Father's glory.[19] David's physical attributes are figures of Christ's spiritual attributes.

Ambiguities or complexities in the words of Scripture about historical matters can signal that something figurative is at work. We noted above the inversion of the historical narrative of David in the order of the psalms. Psalm 71, which in its title says it is about Solomon, states, "justice will arise in his days and abundance of peace until the moon shall cease" and "his dominion will be from sea to sea." The difficulty is that these words do not actually apply to the historical kingdom of Solomon. Something is here that exceeds the reality, indeed the capacity, of Solomon. Precisely in this disjunction of signification and reality, the psalmist points us to a figure: "Therefore," St. Thomas concludes, "this Psalm about the reign of Solomon is to be explained insofar as it is a figure of the reign of Christ, in whom all the things said in the Psalm will be fulfilled." On the other hand, the king signified in "God, give your judgment to the king" (also Psalm 71) could be Solomon; such would not be historically false. In that case, it could signify Solomon and Solomon could in turn be a figure for Christ, for it applies to Christ as well.[20] For St. Thomas, the principle is clear: if a passage is saying something about someone (in this case, Solomon) that is not true of him, then it is to be applied

---

[19] *In Psalmos* 2 (Parma ed., 14:150, no. 2).
[20] For both instances, see *In Psalmos*, prooemium (Parma ed., 14:149).

solely to the one who is being figured (in this case, Christ). If the passage is saying something true of the figure and of the one figured, it can be applied to both.[21]

The Holy Spirit has seen to the writing of Scripture in such a way that things are said that exceed the history and thus lift the soul to what is being figured by the persons and deeds of history. Such passages signify historical persons and events, but because there is something that is not fully and perfectly literal, a deeper signification of the whole is suggested to the commentator. The letter itself makes known the deeper signification of the things. Is the reading literal or spiritual? Figures seem to provide instances that are not necessarily clear as to whether the reading is literal or spiritual. Although St. Thomas is quite clear in principle, in practice he does not seem particularly concerned to make such determinations consistently in his commentaries.

To return to the end and style of the Psalter as prayer, figure further specifies that end. One has concrete historical circumstances in the person of David. At the same time, in that person, one has the figure of Christ, both head and members. These are the prayers of David; as David is a figure of Christ, these are also the prayers of Christ and his Church. The prayers of the first fifty psalms, prayers under persecution and attack, are not just about temporal things but also about spiritual things, for these are the prayers of the penitent, of those under attack by spiritual forces of ill, not just material forces of ill. For the Christian, these prayers not only embrace the fullness

---

[21] *Super Heb* 1:5, lec. 3, Marietti no. 51.

of life in tribulation but unite the Christian with him who is praying, and that is not simply David but Christ and his Church of whom David is a figure. The words are of David and also of Christ and the Church, and therefore of those who are members of Christ's body. Such, for St. Thomas, is the experience of him who reads the Psalms. St. Thomas speaks of singing the Psalms, for he thinks of the Psalms in the context of prayer and especially of the sung communal prayer of the Church.

Isaiah

The mode or style of the prophet occupies a particular place in St. Thomas's understanding of Scripture. To understand it, let us turn again to St. Thomas's prologue to his commentary on Isaiah, which begins with this verse from Habakkuk: "Write down the vision and explain it on tablets so that he who reads it will finish the race because what is seen is still far off but will appear in the end" (Hab 2:2–3). The subject matter of Isaiah, the appearance of Christ, is in the opening command, "write down the vision." St. Thomas says the style is in the second command, "explain it on tablets." The prophet must do more than write or report; he must explain.

The mark of the prophet as human author is vision: the prophet is shown something by God.[22] What is the nature of this vision? The vision could be given to the senses; it could be given to the imagination. Most perfectly, the vision is given to the intellect, and to say that the prophet sees the vision with his intellect is to say that what he sees is beyond images.

---

[22] For what follows, see *Super Isa* 1:1 (Leonine ed., 28:8–9).

Vision here is a metaphor. Vision is proper to the sense of sight, and so we apply it metaphorically to a particular aspect of the intellect. When we understand something, we say, "I see!" We could be working hard to understand it, struggling to make sense of it. We say we are "in the dark." When we see it, we say "the light goes on." That makes sense, since we need light to see. We apply this experience of the senses to intellectual knowing, to grasping things that are not most properly of the senses. The prophet sees with his intellect something shown to him by God. Most perfectly, for St. Thomas, the prophet both sees and understands; they go together for St. Thomas. That which is seen is to be understood. This is the realm of *sententia*, of idea. Such is the nature of the prophetic vision.

What is it the prophet sees? He sees the future. Does that mean events of history? Yes, but that is not at the heart of what is seen by the prophet. St. Thomas distinguishes three ways in which one can see, or know, intellectually. One can know in the light of reason, which is the natural condition of man as a rational animal. One can know in the light of faith, which is the condition of the believer. And one can know in the light of glory, which is the condition of the blessed in heaven. The vision of the prophet is a vision of God but not the vision of glory. The prophet sees God, but from a precise vantage point: "insofar as God is the reason of those things which pertain to the disposition of men in the world."[23] The prophet sees the future, but he does so not just as events that will happen. He sees them precisely within the divine reason, meaning the

---

[23] *Super Isa* 1:1 (Leonine ed., 28:9).

divine intelligibility and ordering of men in the world. The prophet sees something of divine providence in the mind of God precisely as divine providence, not merely as event. He sees intellectually, meaning he grasps something of the divine disposition of man in this world with his intellect. This is what he sees, and this is the matter of the vision and thus the matter of his prophecy.

This helps explain why St. Thomas can say that, although Isaiah speaks in a concrete historical time and place to which St. Thomas is indeed attentive, the matter of the prophet is, in fact, the appearance of Christ. The prophet sees not just events but the order and reason of the disposition of men, and that means he sees how things are ordered to Christ and his three-fold appearance to men.

The prophet is to communicate this vision that has been granted intellectually. In the command in the passage of Habakkuk, the prophet is to "explain" the vision.[24] How he does this falls under style, and for Isaiah this is threefold. First, he explains by way of adaptation of likenesses to the vision. Isaiah is particularly skilled in grasping sensible objects that bear beautiful likenesses to the visions he is communicating. Likenesses are necessary for us because it is natural to our reason to use sensible objects in knowing. With likenesses, man grasps more insightfully those things whose likenesses he perceives with his senses. Isaiah is especially skilled in finding the likenesses that are expressive of what God has shown him intellectually.

---

24 For what follows, see *Super Isa*, prol. (Leonine ed., 28:3–4).

The second way Isaiah explains is in his stating the *sententia* of the vision. We could say he gives the meaning of the vision but understood as the idea that has been shown in the vision and is being expressed in the likenesses. The *sententia* is fundamentally Christ. St. Thomas quotes St. Jerome that Isaiah seems to have produced not a prophecy but a gospel. Such is the clarity of his explanations of the visions.

The third aspect of his explanation is the beauty of his words. Here Thomas again quotes St. Jerome: "He was a man of noble and urbane eloquence." This matters because, in the words of Proverbs, "the tongue of the wise man makes knowledge beautiful" (Prov 15:2).

Intrinsic to Isaiah's style is likeness. This is not just Isaiah; this is the style of prophets. In his commentary on Jeremiah, St. Thomas says the proper style of the prophets is likenesses and figures, which follows from the office of the prophet.[25] With the prophets, we return more precisely to the idea of figure in the reading of Scripture.

As suggested by its place in the style of prophetic speech and writing, a figure points to something else as a way of learning about or knowing that something else. I, for one, enjoyed drawing geometrical figures in geometry class. And then we were told that the figure we were drawing was not really a triangle, but a picture of a triangle, a figure. A triangle is most properly an idea of which there are many figures. Much human learning follows a similar pattern: moving from particulars in our sense experience, to figures (patterns), to ideas. Much of modern science functions in

---

[25] *In Jer*, prooemium (Parma ed., 14:578).

this way. Such is at work in St. Thomas's understanding of corporeal figures to speak about heavenly realities. The prophet has seen something intellectual and must find a figure for it, something that is like it that can serve as the basis for bringing his reader to an understanding of what he has seen. This is what teachers generally do in bringing students from what they know to what they do not know: they find something known that bears some patterned resemblance to what is not known. This especially is what the prophet is to do; thus his style is of likeness and figure.

The Literal Signification of Christ in the Old Testament

What is the relationship between figure and the literal and mystical senses of Scripture? In a case such as David signifying Christ, we have an instance of the mystical sense: the word signifies David, and David signifies Christ. Prophecy can be trickier. The prophet communicates what he sees by way of figure, and certainly in the case of Isaiah what he sees is Christ. How does the signification work? Often times for St. Thomas, the signification is indeed literal. The words signify Christ. There is no need to find some other thing that in turn signifies Christ. Given what we have seen of St. Thomas's understanding of Scripture, this should come as no surprise. The prophecy of Isaiah 7:14—"Behold a virgin shall conceive and bring forth a son"—is literally about Christ; that is, the words signify the birth of Jesus Christ. "This is a sign of the Incarnation of Christ."[26] St. Thomas says these words

---

[26] *Super Isa* 7:14 (Leonine ed., 28:56). See also *Super Matt* 1:23, lec. 5, Marietti no. 148: "It is to be known that, in the Old Testament some passages refer to Christ and are said of him alone, as 'Behold a virgin shall conceive and bring forth a son.'"

"expressly" contain the truth.[27] In the case of prophecy, this is an explanation of the very meaning, the *sententia*, of the prophecy by the prophet. St. Thomas sees Psalm 21—"They divided my vestments among them"—in the same way, as signifying Christ, not David.[28] Prophets also speak in figurative expressions that literally refer to Christ. "A shoot shall come from the stump of Jesse" is literally about Christ, as the words signify him, but by way of figure.[29] Such is the figurative language of the prophet that is literal in its signification of Jesus Christ. The principle is important to St. Thomas: Christ can be spoken of literally in the Old Testament. That no words signify Christ—they only signify things that signify Christ—is the position of Theodore of Mopsuestia, a position, St. Thomas notes, condemned as heretical.[30]

◆

To consider a literary work precisely as literary is to consider its genre and style and the many subsidiary features of each. St. Thomas's understanding of form embraces all of these as giving a unity to the work as literary. Such informs how one is to read a given book in its ordering of the subject matter to its end. St. Thomas finds the richness of genres and styles in Scripture. This is hardly surprising, given what he understands the end and subject of Scripture to be. It

---

[27] *Super Iob* 4:12 (Leonine ed., 26:30).
[28] *In Psalmos*, prooemium (Parma ed., 14:149).
[29] *Super Iob* 4:12 (Leonine ed., 26:30).
[30] See *In Psalmos*, prooemium (Parma ed., 14:149), and *Super Matt* 1:13, lec. 5, Marietti no. 148.

makes sense that a wide range of genres and styles would be used by a variety of authors. The subtlety of his understanding of the human authors, especially his understanding of prophecy, only deepens his appreciation of the forms of Sacred Scripture and his attention to them.

CONCLUSION

St. Thomas's genius is marked not only by the extraordinary breadth and depth of what he knew but by his ability to give all of it order. He helps his readers understand any number of specific things about God or man or other creatures, but that understanding is always shaped by an understanding of the order and relation of those things he knows. He articulates all of this in his unfailingly lean and precise prose (and poetry). This, of course, is what he understood to be the task of the wise man.

All of this is true of his reading of Sacred Scripture. We find in St. Thomas a capacious understanding of Scripture that is not his own. He inherited it, but he made it his own. Perhaps because he shares the fundamentals with his contemporaries and his forebears, his holy teachers, he does not dedicate a work simply to the nature and reality of Scripture. Instead, he comments on Scripture and, in so doing, opens up for us his own clear articulation of the tradition he has inherited. As is so often the case, his articulation helps us better understand the very thing he has articulated. The student of St. Thomas must, however, read widely in his work to see the expansiveness of his understanding of Scripture. I have sought in this book to present as simply and clearly as I can the expansive ways in which St. Thomas understands Scripture and how that in turn shapes his reading of it.

Some of his language is technical to his time, and I have sought to clarify it for the modern reader. Such, for example, is the language of causality that, when we can see what St. Thomas means, retains its value in the hands of so skilled an expositor of reality. I have sought to clarify those areas that could prove confusing to modern readers, such as what St. Thomas means by a "literal" reading of Scripture or what he means by "intention."

Fundamentally, I sought to bring out St. Thomas's deepest vision of Scripture. I think it is the vision of the holy teachers, as St. Thomas would call them, and indeed the vision of the Church. I say this not to close off the many modern advances in the study of Scripture. I have no doubt that there is much in modern scholarship that would simply delight St. Thomas. At the same time, he would have a clear sense of what to do with it, of its place in a well-ordered whole. He would bring his wisdom to bear. It is a wisdom that is perennially useful and fresh.